Early Praise From Business Owners, Managers and Change Professionals

"Use the tools and exercises David Winkelman offers in *Embracing Change From the Inside Out* and forever change your life!"

Marshall Goldsmith –
International best-selling author or editor of 35 books
including What Got You Here Won't Get You There and Triggers.

Once we begin to see, and learn that we're not on this earth to control the things that never stop changing around us, but rather allow these moments to show us the need to change the view of life we hold within us . . . then we are on the right path towards discovering and fulfilling the true purpose of our lives. In clear-cut style, Mr. Winkelman provides many helpful clues as to "how" we can actualize this new and higher self-understanding.

— Guy Finley, Author of the best-selling *Secret of Letting Go*

"Once we have established a successful routine, change (even for the better) is one of life's great challenges. David has shared in his book, *Embracing Change*, practical tools, warmth and humor, to help each of us make better choices for our own life satisfaction, and to have more empathy for others who struggle with these concepts. I love the way this book feels like a loving conversation with caring mentor, instead of a 'how to'".

Marguerite Lorenz, Executive Director, EstatePlanning101.org

"For those who wholeheartedly choose to engage with the insights and exercises contained here, this book promises to deliver life-changing application."

Mark Yeeles, Relational Wisdom 360

"David Winkelman knows change from the inside out because it is a journey he has taken himself. If you're ready for a life changing journey, read and apply this book."

Laura Hansen
Retired CEO and Executive Coach, Center for Creative Leadership

In Embracing Change, David Winkelman offers a uniquely creative approach to respond to the ups and downs of work and life with humor and insight. Winkelman's intelligent and distinctive perspective makes change feel like a worthwhile adventure.

Sandy Asch,
Bestselling Author,
ROAR: How to Build a Resilient Organization the World Famous San Diego Zoo Way"

Should you read this book? Absolutely! How rare a treat to find a book that gives you relatable stories, and tools that you can actually use. It delivers on the promise of the title."

Jeff Perlis, Real Estate Broker

"Winkelman is the consummate professional among sherpas who can help guide those who are ready to achieve desired change. His book is a must read for anyone wanting to grasp the challenges of the inner change process. It will help you transform the beliefs and behaviors that are inhibiting desired change into breakthrough and success in what is one of the most difficult arenas in life."

Greg Voisen, Founder, Inside Personal Growth, www.insidepersonalgrowth.com

"This book works! Winkelman offers an extremely practical doable model for change. He does a great job motivating readers to take action and giving them effective tools to ensure their success."

Andrew Oser, Owner, Mount Shasta Retreat

"Change is an inevitable and constant experience in our personal, professional, emotional and physical lives. Adapting to change is one of most essential skills we can learn. *Embracing Change* is one of the most honest, realistic and applicable approaches I have seen in a book on change. Winkelman takes us through an interactive journey that will help create actual shifts in our thought process and teaches us doable skills for every aspect of our lives.

I highly recommend this book for any organizations of two or more. It will help any reader make the right decisions, avoid the wrong decisions and embrace the constant change in the culture in which he or she lives."

Lisa Lapides Sawicki, Certified Life Coach

EMBRACING CHANGE

FROM THE INSIDE OUT

Game-Changing Options For
Transforming Self, Team and Company

DAVID B. WINKELMAN

Winkelman
SOLUTIONS
Making Desired Change Easier

www.winkelmansolutions.com

Embracing Change From The Inside Out:
Game-Changing Options For Transforming Self, Team and Company
by David B. Winkelman

Published By:
Winkelman Solutions
10367 Agar Ct.
San Diego, CA 92126
www.winkelmansolutions.com
david@winkelmansolutions.com

Cover design by Raffy Ferras Hoylar at GSPH and David Winkelman
Interior layout and design by David Winkelman
All visuals and photographs are by David Winkelman, except those on the cover (in part) and on pages: iii, iv, vi, 6, 7, 12, 18, 33, 41, 54, 59, 62, 63 (3 silhouettes), 64, 83, 84, 88, 92, 96, 98, 108, 109, 110, 111, 113, 115, 124, 128, 139, 160 – all of which were downloaded, whose permissions are not readily known or pending, and many of which have been modified beyond recognition.

The author does not dispense medical advice or prescribe the use of any technique as a form of treatment for physical, psychological, or medical problems or conditions. Readers should seek their own advice and treatment from a physician or qualified mental health professional. The suggestions contained in this book are for your information only. The publisher and author assume no responsibility for actions taken by others.

ISBN: 978-0-9976315-0-0
Winkelman, David B., 1954-

Embracing Change From The Inside Out: Game-Changing Options For Transforming Self, Team and Company
1. Business   2. Management   3. Change   4. Transformation   5. Personal Growth

First printing 2016
Printed in the United States of America

DEDICATIONS

To my wife, Doretta, who's been infinitely patient with my own transformation.

To the very best in you and your connection to the force or people who bring it out in you.

ACKNOWLEDGEMENTS

My deep thanks to . . .

. . . My parents, Alice, Stuart and Sally, for your enormous support over the years, especially in the hard times.

. . . The handful of role models I've been fortunate to know well in my life: My brother, Marc, lifelong friend, Andy Lipkis, former employer Mark Chapparone; supporters Mark Yeeles and Bruno Seemann, in clients who challenged me, Sandy Asch, Matt and Gail Taylor, Patsy Kahoe, Michael Kaufman and Bryan Coffman, who taught me much of my craft and its potential for fun and life-changing contribution.

. . . Friends who believed in me and actively supported me through challenging times: Tom and Trisha Kelly, Nancy Nell, Peter Kane, David and Lori Libs, Jeff Perlis, Joe Sterling, Aubrey Ward, Dave Brown, John and Jan Atkinson, Kate Lipkis, our 6-Day Group and Wayne Williams.

. . . My clients, who gave me the opportunity to learn, grow, produce and make a difference in their own change process.

. . . Book consultant Victoria Vinton, editors Adrienne Moch and Rick Lineback, and those who read and gave me advice with this book, Gregg Ward, Greg Voisen, Scott Ramey, Jill Wasserstrom, Jeff Perlis, Maggie Cadman, Krista Lombardi, Paul Silver, Tom Meredith, Lisa Lapides Sawicki, Helen Davis, Laura Hansen, Mark Yeeles, Martha Warriner Jarrett, Sabrina Must, Marguerite Lorenz, and Doretta Winkelman.

. . . Robin Edgar for your wonderful cartoon characters and willingness to collaborate so tightly on the details, and Raffy Hoylar, my cover co-designer. Finally, to the handful of uncredited photographers who created the images I pulled from the Internet.

PREFACE

Achieving desired change can be a gnarly process for people and organizations. If only there was a book or kernel of wisdom that by itself could bring it about! As the primary driver of self-change in our lives, each of us must pursue it with determination and effective action. This appears to happen naturally and joyfully as we grow up; then gradually, as we age, that joy we feel can give way to comfort, protection and fear.

Embracing Change is an opportunity to *step back* from, *take stock* of and possibly *reset* some of your own change habits and attitudes. It offers a framework that will help you recognize how the behavior patterns you generate on the inside produce the situations you deal with on the outside, and help you create the growth you're looking for.

INTENDED TAKEAWAYS — WHAT'S IN IT FOR YOU?

As a result of reading this book, you can:

1) Increase your self-awareness.
2) Think differently about the possibility for desired change.
3) See some kinds of discomfort as opportunities for growth.
4) Engage others and seek support from them, so you're not just clanking around in your own head about things.
5) Recognize yours and other's readiness for desired change, or a lack of it.
6) Implement the GameChanger approach for getting a grasp on any desired change.

Change is a huge and serious subject, so I wanted to approach it with as much lightness, creativity and personality as I could. Most of the visuals in the book are my own creation. I've offered myself and my own change process as an example. If *Embracing Change* makes a difference in your life, please email me (you'll find address at the end of this book) so we can celebrate your wins! If you would like support in using this material, especially in dealing with any challenges you may encounter, I'm available as a coach, trainer and consultant.

CONTENTS

The design of this book is intended to make it as interactive as possible and thus more valuable to you. It features:

- A simple system: The Five GameChangers
- 15 exercises spread throughout the book
- Questions at the start of each of the Five GameChanger chapters
- Visuals throughout the book created mostly by the author
- Sidebars in which to make notes as you read

You'll find an overview a list of all the perspective sections on pages 142-143.

FOREWORD

*"It is not the strongest of the species that survives,
nor the most intelligent that survives.
It is the one that is most adaptable to change."*

Charles Darwin

If Darwin was correct in his premise, why is it humans have such a difficult time changing behaviors?

I recently attended a symposium at Harvard on affordable housing. One of the very last speakers put forward the provocation that "the reason we have an affordable housing crisis is that we have chosen not to fix it." In others words, he went on to say, "...we know what the solutions are. We just choose not to act on them." It was quite a startling comment given I was in the midst of reading David Winkelman's manuscript *Embracing Change*. In quick order, I was struck by the notion that the biggest inhibitor to change is usually observed by looking in the mirror.

Embracing Change attempts to provide a clear, complete and fun guide to changing one's behaviors. Much of what will happen in the next few decades is inevitable and will be driven by forces already in motion today. David Winkelman provides an optimistic road map that allows its followers to break from the inevitable and to chart a new course by crafting a narrative for change.

Embracing Change cracks the code of inertia and shows us how to change. Winkelman provides readers numerous exercises that demonstrate how to use his GameChangers in real time. The exercises are probing and lead to clarity of purpose, an identification of the obstacles to change and how to overcome them. The tools he provides are simple to use and fun.

Through practical techniques and integrated visual exercises, he offers readers a new perspective — namely, how we can make a difference by embracing change and inspiring others to become believers in their own ability to shape the future, as opposed to being victimized by it. In the spirit of his request that as you read his work you allow yourself to be vulnerable, I chose as my goal in one of the exercises to lose 10 pounds. Winkelman forced me to confront the stark reality of what was preventing me from losing weight. It was the person I look at in the mirror every day. I know what the solution is. I was choosing not to adapt my own behavior in order to achieve the goal. I can say with confidence if I stay the course he asks me to travel, I almost certainly will succeed in the next two months.

I know of no other book on change that better teaches readers how to take charge of their own destiny. Imagine what life would be like if you had expertise that enabled you to continuously adapt to the ever-increasing dynamics of our interconnected world!

Tom Meredith

Former CFO of Dell, Inc.; Investor; Community Activist; and Collector of Friends

Austin, Texas

Heraclitus, Greek philosopher
535 - 475 BC

INTRODUCTION

I created *Embracing Change* as a unique interactive experience. Imagine reaching into your pocket and discovering a tiny magic lamp that's home to a genie, who specializes in personal change. He'll grant you any three wishes for making personal changes you want, but suggests that you'll have to work a little to achieve those changes. The genie, of course, is a metaphor for the awareness and power within you that can help you achieve almost any desired changes you want. Do you make the wishes or pass on the opportunity? What's at stake could be a breakthrough: one you've likely wanted.

Given how many books on the subject of change there are, I wanted this one to be imme-diately practical and easy to use. I therefore designed it to provide:

- A more visual and personal approach to helping achieve almost any change.
- An experience that nudges you to take action while reading it.
- Plenty of options and reference points.

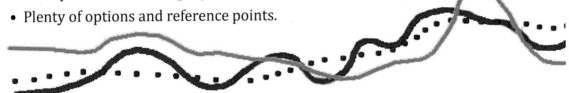

How can we make strides in our personal growth easier? We know that life doesn't look like lines on a graph. It's messy, slippery and in our face. Pressure points shift constantly. My aim is to help make the kinds of change or growth you desire within yourself, team or company faster, more predictable and real enough for you to make it happen.

In Chapter 1, to help lay a foundation for your own personal experience of this mate-rial, I share some revealing personal pieces of my own change story — things that aren't easy to talk about. As we move through the book, I want to connect with your *feelings* as much as your intellect. That's how your greatest potential can be unlocked.

Chapter 2 provides an overview about personal change — illustrating that life *IS* change — so we better be as prepared for and skilled at change as possible for it's a critical success factor. On the second page of this chapter, I ask what would you like to change in yourself. I suggest you pick one thing in particular as a way to make your reading of the book all the more relevant and valuable.

Chapter 3 introduces my own approach to problem solving and achieving desired change quickly using the Five GameChangers[1]. To visually represent what I see as the major components of the entire desired change process, I created the five unique characters shown here. As a team, these desired change *superheroes* provide a simple system for integrating over 100 perspectives on desired and self-driven change found throughout the book.

In chapters four through eight, we'll delve into the many ways each of the Five GameChangers can work for you. Beginning with Clarity (the longest chapter) and ending with Action, we'll look at a wide variety of options, perspectives and examples.

Chapter 9 concludes with a panoramic scan of "What's Next": options for implementation and follow-through designed to supercharge your success using all you've learned.

EXPLORING THE LANDSCAPE OF DESIRED CHANGE

Another way to think of this book is as a road map through the landscape of desired change — or a kind of territory flyover — with more potential routes than you can count. Ideally, you'll spot some good places to land, where you might tromp around the local terrain, get dirty and emerge with a new and  different perspective. Doing the 15 simple exercises I've provided along the way and answering the questions I ask here and there, will set you up for expanding your skills at self-change. The lined side-bars from pages 1-139 are there for you to note any takeaways, insights or questions that might further support your learning or action.

As illustrated in the doodle below, our real-life journey through this landscape can vary widely. The straightest possible path I know is to learn and use the Five GameChangers in chapters four through eight. By making them yours and practicing the approach I offer a little bit every day, they'll become a part of your change skill set in a short time.

WHERE YOU ARE NOW (A) — **WHERE YOU WANT TO BE (Z)**

Another way to think of this book is as a manual for getting unstuck and becoming less automatic. The less we're bound by habitual and ineffective behavior, the more we access our true potential. This process can release us from limitation, whether it's a harmful real-world situation or what might feel like a self-imposed internal jail cell.

As suggested by *An Autobiography in Five Short Chapters* on the following page, whatever form of stuck is on your mind, from a specific frustration to not feeling enough joy in life, at some point you'll probably find yourself being more honest about it. Why not get there faster and start today?

AN AUTOBIOGRAPHY IN FIVE SHORT CHAPTERS* Portia Nelson

1.
I walk down the street.
There is a deep hole in the sidewalk.
I fall in.
I am lost ... I am helpless.
It isn't my fault.

2.
I walk down the same street.
There is a deep hole in the sidewalk.
I pretend I don't see it.
I fall in again.
I can't believe I am in the same place.
But it isn't my fault.
It still takes a long time to get out.

3.
I walk down the same street.
There is a deep hole in the sidewalk.
I see it is there.
I still fall in ... it's a habit ... but,
My eyes are open.
I know where I am.
It is my responsibility.
I get out immediately.

4.
I walk down the same street.
There is a deep hole in the sidewalk.
I walk around it.

5.
I walk down another street.

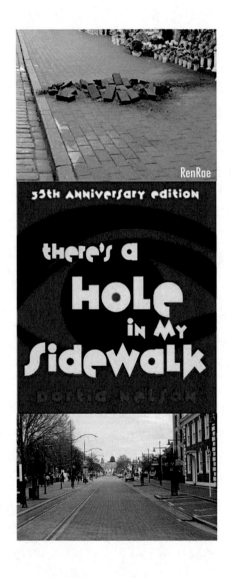

RenRae

35th Anniversary edition

there's a
Hole
in my
Sidewalk

Portia Nelson

* This poem is well-circulated and easy-to-find on the Internet.

CLOSING THE GAP BETWEEN KNOWING AND DOING

As you read, you may find yourself thinking: *I already know that* — and you might! The aim here is to create a shift by leveraging[2] what you already know and experience. To get the most value from this book, I invite you to continually ask three questions:

1. How can I grasp the idea and apply it to a shift I'm seeking?
2. What action can I take toward my desired behavior?
3. How might I be creating or allowing an obstacle to a change I want?

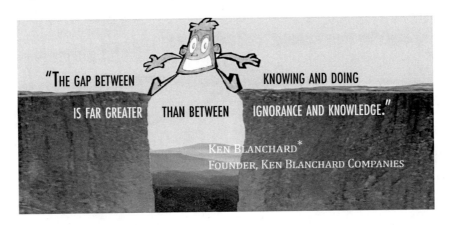

"THE GAP BETWEEN KNOWING AND DOING IS FAR GREATER THAN BETWEEN IGNORANCE AND KNOWLEDGE."

KEN BLANCHARD*
FOUNDER, KEN BLANCHARD COMPANIES

By digging into *Embracing Change* as an interactive experience, you'll get far more than additional information or knowledge. You'll get to explore *yourself being* your best! May the experience last a lifetime and be fun along the way!

There's also a chance that some of what you read here may stir up a little discomfort. That's good. It's part of the process, so expect it. Know that by "leaning into" your discomfort — acknowledging it, not running from it, perhaps talking about it, breathing or laughing through it — you become a stronger change practitioner every day.

*Ken is co-author of the *One Minute Manager*, author of 40 business books and founding partner of The Ken Blanchard Companies, a global training company. This quote is from one of his many public speeches.

OUR POTENTIAL FOR SELF-CHANGE

In the diagram below you'll see a representation of three related domains. Each domain contains variables that affect our behavior. The grey zone in the middle (though hardly proportional,) represents the possibility for personal change. The potential for playing in that zone is enormous — much greater than it actually looks.

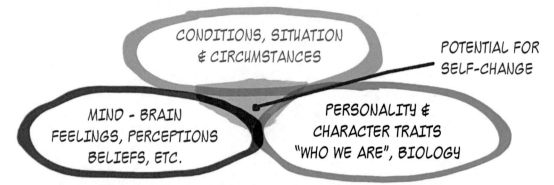

Hundreds (if not thousands) of different systems in the world for understanding and predicting behavior aim to expand this grey *growth zone*. Some of these systems you might know by name, like Abraham Maslow's "Hierarchy of Needs.", the Meyers-Briggs, DISC, and NLP (Neuro-Linguistic Programming) as taught and practiced by Anthony Robbins — to name just a few. There are so many it makes my head spin.

Change is most likely when we allow it or pursue it with determination, and the conditions are right for it. Sometimes we have to alter or create our situations when those conditions are not yet right *enough*.

In writing this book, I set out to actualize my own potential for change. I wanted to:

1) shift some of my own behaviors in ways I wasn't previously able;

2) get better and faster at making changes — be more adaptable;

3) reach more people and make the biggest positive difference I could.

Along the way I discovered a great deal that I hadn't fully understood or experienced before. Much of what I learned I share here and strive to put into practice every day.

1
MY OWN CHANGE STORY

When an associate suggested I needed to write a book, I took it as a sign and jumped in. Little did I know all it would require and what I would go through to get there. From the start I wanted to write about the process of internal change. The book would creatively explore how *each of us* can make desired change more skillfully when we see ourselves as practitioners of change in a culture of change. What I didn't foresee was the transformative experience I, too, would have along the way.

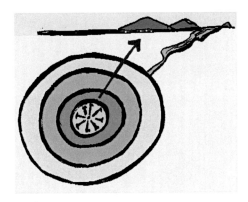

We'll begin with a pivotal life-changing story for me — about how I unexpectedly came to buy my first house at age 33. I was a month into a new job, driving with my new employer. In less time than it took for a light to change, he said something that began to transform my life. He shared a perspective that convinced me that I needed to buy a home. *What?!?* At that point in my life, my wife and I had burdened ourselves with $20,000 in credit card debt, and had almost no savings. Financially things did not look good for us. Until then, I'd presumed that eventually, some-day, we would be able to buy a home, but that option wasn't real

Embracing Change is about how each of us can make desired change more skillfully, by seeing ourselves as practitioners of change in a culture of change.

1

to me prior to that point. Home buying was what most *other* people did and I didn't see it in our immediate future. My boss's perspective shifted my reality in a way that I had to take action immediately. In that moment, I stopped thinking of myself as a renter and switched to thinking of myself as an owner. Before I knew what had happened, I'd let go of my old self-perception.

My new employer was a year younger than me, a tradesman and entrepreneur who had graduated high school with an equivalency test. Yet he already owned five businesses and several homes, and had a family. His exact words were: "David, you're not on the financial map until you own a home." BAM! In seconds, those few words triggered[3] a game-changing shift in my thinking. It flipped me into a state of being willing to do whatev-

er it took to make that happen. Over the course of the next 10 months, we found, bought and moved into our home. The process filled me with a greater sense of responsibility and financial presence than I'd ever experienced before. The story illustrates an essential message of this book:

It can take only moments to shift our perceptions. When that happens, our beliefs, our behavior and our results will follow.

That shift in my own perception narrowed what I call the "potential-versus-actual gap"[4] that most of us live in to one degree or an-

> Most of us live in our own potential-versus-actual gap, but we generally don't talk about it with others.

other. I was more than fortunate to have had an employer who took the time to have that discussion with me and alter my home owning trajectory — no doubt by years. What was critical to achieving that change was talking honestly about my situation with him, and to do that I had to trust him enough that it would move me in the right direction.

Transformation has been my life's work for over 30 years. This focus first began taking shape from 1974-77 at UCLA, as a participant in the Creative Problem Solving Program. My interest in transformation grew into a passion over the next 20 years as I worked in a series of high-stress management positions and engaged with Fortune 100 companies. I've been fortunate to know and work with some extraordinary people. I've been married to the same amazing woman for 31 years. I practice yoga and have taught breathing methods to corporate teams. I laugh and create as many moments of joy as possible, allow tears to roll when I'm moved, and I appreciate the miracle of my existence a little more each day.

Then there's that *other* side of me, where, over the course of my life I unwittingly sabotaged myself more times than I want to admit. I lost touch with key parts of myself so early in life I got used to living in a huge potential-versus-actual gap. This book reflects my narrowing that gap by replacing limiting behavior patterns with empowering ones. To narrow that gap, I had to root out those limiting patterns, first by clearly seeing and owning them.

> In some way shape or form, transformation has been my life's work for over 30 years.

GETTING TO THE ROOTS

By the time I was two, my parents, both in their early 20's, were on the road to divorce, yelling at one another and sometimes at me. It was traumatic to me. Unconsciously, I thought I could lessen the stress and tension in and around me by being agreeable and appealing, presenting as few emotional demands of my own — in essence receding. I tried to create a sense of safety and acceptance by behaving in a way I thought made them happy — or at least *less upset*. In always having to be "good" in the presence my primary relationships, I grew to become emotionally detached from myself. I wouldn't grasp the long-term effects of doing this

and the cost to my own self-acceptance — for decades.*

Odd as it may sound, people who experience childhood trauma[5] don't always know it. I didn't. Being smart and operating intellectually[6] was my chief way of coping. I could disappear into my mind, stay relatively numb to my body and my emotions, say the right things, and look good. In doing this, I barely knew what my real feelings were. Living from an overwhelming sense of "have to," I did what I thought others wanted, rarely giving myself the time, attention, respect or acceptance I now know is healthy. By always having answers and helping others solve their problems, I managed to do fairly well in my career, too — until a crisis hit.

> I wouldn't grasp the real and long-term effects of this social pattern for decades.

* No implication is intended that patterns I describe in this chapter apply to either you or *most people*. It can be worthwhile to discover what you *can't see* that might be holding you back. The answer to being stuck is not always as simple as: Apply more willpower. It might be time to discover and do something about an unknown or unconscious negative X-factor if one is operating in you.

IS THIS REALLY HAPPENING?

In early 2007, the Great Recession rolled through my workplace and, like so many others, I was laid off from a comfortable management position. In response to my job loss, and to deal with other unproductive behaviors, I began weekly coaching sessions with a psychologist. At the end of a year, he told me I had a general anxiety disorder.* *What?!* How was it possible that prior to this I'd never considered the possibility of anxiety as the condition I'd spent so much of my life reacting to? For me, anxiety had simply been my state of "normal."

In navigating my life situation-by-situation, the deep changes I needed to make were long delayed. My ability to rationalize, along with a great passion for things *outside* me,[7] masked the anxiety. Externally I could function at an acceptable level, but internally I was pre-occupied with and constrained by constant stress. While the process rendered me less effective than I knew I could be, I continued through life *coping* with what the universe seemed to be dishing out. I couldn't see the way in which I was contributing to one situation after another.

As blind spots and denial clouded my clarity, I protected myself with excuses, justification and emotionally numbing.[8] I avoided what made me uneasy. It was actually a challenge for me to say, "That makes me uncomfortable."

> He said I had a general anxiety disorder.

* It had never come up in the coaching or in any other conversation, either.

UNRAVELING A STATE OF STUCK

We don't always wake up when the alarm goes off. I sure didn't. But over time, I came to understand how the processes known as "emotional hijacking"[9] was affecting my thinking and behavior. The entire pattern had been operating as a blind spot in me for years.[10]

When the childhood trauma from which my anxiety sprung finally become clear to me, I sought and received the kind of professional support I needed to heal it.[11] Understanding the unconscious motivation that drove my actions, and taking responsibility for these patterns began my recovery and transformation. I don't believe anyone freely chooses to be stuck and frustrated, yet it seems to happen a lot, as we know and will explore further. Not recognizing and owning your state of stuck definitely makes it worse.

LAUGHTER AND LETTING GO

Yes, it's difficult to look at the invisible and painful issues that keep us feeling limited, yet to progress and grow we must. This often means letting go of something — which we humans often seem to have difficulty doing. Rather than judging or avoiding it, let's get on with it. Laughter can make it easier and faster. If I were there with you in person, we would likely be laughing already.

This is why understanding your own intrinsic motivation, through the fourth GameChanger, is critical.

2
LIFE IS CHANGE

Change is happening everywhere, so it's best to be as ready as possible for it. In this chapter, we'll explore your outlook on self-change and see how ready you are for it. Take note of your response to the following story about two friends of mine, Jerry and Kathy, a retired couple with grown children, living in the white, conservative, prosperous community of Coronado, CA.

In 2001, the couple decided they would alter their lives by sharing their home with a group of four refugees from Africa. For five years, four "Lost Boys" from genocide-ravaged Southern Sudan, airlifted by the U.S. government as part of the largest resettlement program in U.S. history, lived in their home. Jerry and Kathy, meanwhile, moved into the guest house behind their home, forgoing hundreds of thousands of dollars in potential guest house revenue and funding the living expenses of their guests. There, the four young men grew up and became productive members of U.S. society. For Jerry and Kathy, it turned out to be one of the most rewarding things they ever did, and Jerry says they would "do again in a heartbeat."

> For Jerry and Kathy, it turned out to be one of the most rewarding things they ever did, which he says, they would "do it again in a heartbeat."

I lead with this story to convey an essential message: When you embrace a change with enough clarity and purpose, you *can* do it skillfully, joyfully and with fulfilling results.

San Diego Reader 1/25/07. Permission pending
To better understand their motivation or the ways in which it changed them personally, please read about it at: http://www.sandiegoreader. com/news/2007/jan/25/we-have-tell-story-because-we-survived/#

_____
_____
_____
_____
_____
_____
_____
_____

What would you like to change in yourself?

_____
_____
_____
_____
_____

WHAT WOULD YOU LIKE TO CHANGE IN YOURSELF?

Can you hear a voice inside you saying: I want to . . .

Be more effective?	Eat healthier?
Get a new job?	Get more exercise?
Get to my ideal weight?	Use intuition more?
Create a loving relationship?	Express greater creativity?
Resolve an issue?	Move forward faster?
Forgive someone?	Make more rapid progress?
Make more money?	Express the real me?
Change or end a bad habit?	Be more positive?
Start a positive habit?	Be happier?
Stop procrastinating?	Be more assertive?
Be less reactive?	Be more present?
Relax more?	Be more outgoing?
Start doing yoga?	Increase my income?
Have more free time?	Feel my feelings more?
Let a whole lot of stuff go?	Be a better public speaker?
Develop greater focus?	Identify my vision or purpose?
Feel more confident?	Make new friends?
Have more time for myself?	Transform[12] _____ in my life?

Of course, this list is only a hint of what's possible to change. If one of these items doesn't quite do it for you, create one of your own. If just thinking about picking something feels challenging, that means you're on the right track! There's no right or wrong here. Take your time, notice any discomfort and allow something to emerge. To get the most value from this book, I recommend that you pick one specific and definite thing that you'd like to change, with no judgment about it being good or bad, large, small, etc. Just begin — and know that you can alter it at any time.

Whatever it is, write it down in pencil on the line below. Make it as simple and clear as possible, Throughout this book we'll consider this to be your *desired change*.

My desired behavior change is:

_____

_____

. . . Congratulations if you've identified this change for yourself. If you haven't yet, you can, of course, do that at any time.[13]

In the process of helping you achieve this change, we'll be exploring the many dimensions of our personality and culture that influence the change process. One major aim of this book is to enhance your ability to step back, look at these various dimensions, be your own executive and make optimal choices. The large happy character you see here holding all the smaller characters represents your **Executive Function (EF),** the *presence* or awareness within you that at any point can step in and manage the many co-existing aspects inside you.

This book is about your ability to step back, look at those various dimensions, be your own executive and make optimal choices.

DECIDING TO EMBRACE CHANGE

Why is change so difficult? What makes us decide to change or not to? What gets in the way of self-change? On these next two pages we begin to explore these questions. Answers you may have heard before, like: "I don't need to change badly enough, or "The pain of staying the same doesn't yet exceed the pain of making the change," or "We're just creatures of habit." don't seem to help that much. We need to look deeper.

It's clear we've been gifted brains, bodies and emotional tools designed for a *lifetime of change*. These gifts enable us to think, feel, love, learn, adapt, grow, flex, imagine, create, connect with others, and succeed at almost anything to which we truly dedicate ourselves. All our individual and collective wisdom tells us we can manage our potential behavior changes either *before* — or *after* something bad occurs. Before is preferable, yet we don't always act on that wisdom. Becoming skilled at making desired change faster and more proactively is actually part of our DNA.

Moving through your own landscape of change using any of the perspectives here will accelerate your progress and increase your awareness — especially in dealing with moments of discomfort.

Our collective experience thus makes our choices clearer: We can manage our potential behavior changes in advance of or after something bad happens."

Beginning our journey with questions like, "Why are some desired behavior changes *so* difficult or frightening?" we'll emerge with the understanding that internal change can be a skill that gets easier and faster the more it's practiced. Let's start by looking at some basic ways we think about change.

Sometimes the process of achieving desired change seems at odds with the forces of habit or inertia in us. While we might think of change as *conflict*, generally speaking, most of us don't even operate out of a single mind much of the time. Our brains incorporate at least two very different yet related systems: our rational mind (intellect), and our emotions. The book *SWITCH: How to Change Things When Change is Hard*,[14] illustrates this duality with an analogy to an elephant (our emotions) carrying a rider (our rational mind). As we have long been aware, however, the emotional and rational don't always work in harmony.

RIDER - "control"
Conscious rational mind & intention

ELEPHANT -
Unconscious mind
feelings

PATH - circumstances & situation

> Most of us don't even operate out of a single mind much of the time.

Take for example, how we deal with laws and morals. The Ten Commandments address ten of the all-time greatest potential conflicts between reason and emotional desire: to steal or not to steal, do what is "right" versus "wrong", etc. After more than three millennia, countless people still have issues when it comes to making behavior choices. Options for right, least risky or most tempting ways to behave pull us in different directions. Embracing change means understanding our motivation.

> Often the reality we're dealing with in the moment is one in our mind, and not the same as the reality outside us.

UNDERSTANDING AUTOMATIC

In our quest to embrace change, we'll acknowledge and examine that aspect of our mind we call the unconscious. The following story illustrates the difference between unconscious (and often automatic) thinking and behaving, versus consciously chosen, skillful, optimal behavior. Ideally, we want to sync our internal reality — what's going on inside us — with what's ever-changing outside us.

One day I brought home a full cup of coffee and placed it in the middle of a counter by itself. Later, while moving too quickly, I knocked it over. "So what?" you might ask. "Isn't that just a harmless little mishap?" Sure, but there's more to it: When the reality *in our mind* is a little too out of sync with the reality outside us, that gap or disconnection can create a difficulty of some kind.

The incident points to a significant challenge in changing our behavior: How can we best deal with our unconscious mind, the automatic thinker that governs our habitual and much of our normal thought? It's like that elephant in terms of its power over us.

Is it registering?

If we want to change our behavior — something we're fully capable of doing — then at times we must reduce our *automatic* thinking. What's automatic is what's habitual, often reactive and governed by our unconscious mind. In contrast, what's conscious takes extra time, effort and focus. The *choice* we have is to reduce the automatic. (For me, that would be rushing.) What will *you* focus on?

EXPLORATORY EXERCISE #1 – ASSOCIATIONS

Having taken in a few more ideas about change, let's take another minute to look at what *you* associate with the word change.

In this short experiment. You'll need the following tools:

1) A two-minute timer (which any smartphone has)

2) Something to record your thoughts. Suggestion: Use the margins of this and the facing page.

Here's the process. Read it through before beginning.

1. Set your timer for two minutes.

2. Say the word CHANGE to yourself and see it in your mind.

3. Close your eyes . . . start your timer.

4. Notice what thoughts, feelings, images and sensations come up for you — and how strong they are. Notice where your mind takes you based on this one word — for 120 seconds.

5. Take a minute or more to write down what came up for you.

_____

_____

_____

_____

_____

_____

What do you associate with the word "change"?

Whatever your response, you'll use it at the end of the book. That's why we're documenting it. There are no right answers — just your answers. When you're ready, start writing! Get something down.

> Landscapes, with their large number of potential routes, destinations and experiences, demonstrate many paths to desired change.

SPARKS FOR CHANGE

It takes a spark to light a fire. That's what I want these stories, metaphors or exercises to do for you. Metaphors can help us see things more clearly and emotionally by hitting something "right on the head," or "smack in our face." Landscapes, with their potential routes, destinations and experiences, demonstrate many paths to desired change. Along the way we encounter people, conditions, unexpected wonders and headaches which push us forward. Great relationships can become inspiring, healing or creative forces. What stories might spark some inner growth for *you*? Here's an another example . . .

In 2014, I was part of a corporate change event which demonstrated the utility of changing your point of view. My client, Bob, a former senior officer in the Navy SEALs, was delivering a keynote on SEAL teamwork to a group of Deloitte and Oracle sales executives, alliance partners in a world of high-tech change. To drive home his message about changing a mindset, Bob shared an "old-school" tool, a card that been given to him and other SEAL officers by a four-star general. There, on a big screen, was a simple card showing the executives a new way to expand their thinking. Within seconds you could feel the energy in the room shift . . . By the next morning, those sales execs had already planned a rollout of the card in their own companies.

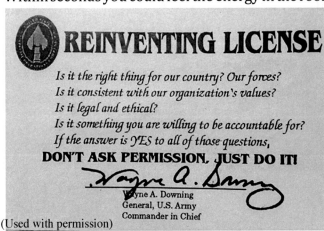

(Used with permission)

EXPLORATORY EXERCISE #2 – FIRST IMPRESSIONS

First, close your eyes and take a few moments to focus on that behavior change you want in your own life, from page 8 - 9.

Then, look at the words below and check off the ones you associate with that change goal. Check any box that applies.

⟳ Tough	⬤ Predictable	△ Political
○ Annoying	❏ Surprising	⟳ Personal
❑ Frightening	⇨ Amusing	✿ Climate
⬛ Avoidable	○ Simple	❏ Unwanted
❏ Unpredictable	⟳ Complex	❑ Desired
✿ Necessary	✋ Immediate	○ Innovation
○ Challenging	△ Long-term	✿ Technology
△ Accelerating	❏ Internal	⬛ Painful
○ Difficult	✿ External	○ Responsibility
⟳ Fun	⇨ Confronting	△ Messed-up
❏ Easy	❏ Inevitable	❑ Inconvenient
⇨ Manageable	○ Funny	⇨ Uncomfortable
✿ Wonderful	❏ Habits	✋ Obstacles
△ Emotional	⬛ Unavoidable	⬛ Roadblocks
⟳ Constant	⟳ Exciting	○ Ruts

How many positive associations did you have? _____

How many negative associations did you have? _____

How many neutral associations did you have? _____

Can you draw any insights or conclusions? _____

_____

How do you think about change in your own life?

How many boxes did you check?

> Change can easily feel overwhelming, and frightening — especially in the moments when we feel alone in it . . . but but we're really living in it all in it together.

The survey is intended to suggest an important idea:
There *might* be a stretch in the very idea of embracing change.

Remember the metaphor of change as landscape on page iii? Here's a second metaphor: Change is an ocean we all live in. Some of us find ourselves in boats of various sizes, feeling relatively safe and secure. Others feel like we're right in the water, thrashing in the waves of intense stress, if not danger. For some, the kinds of change we're talking about might look nearly impossible. For others, the changes will come easier. It often depends on who else is around you and the support they offer.

Given that change is simultaneously personal, organizational, cultural, societal, and global, it can easily feel overwhelming and frightening — especially in the moments when we feel alone in it.

So let's remember that we're not alone; we're really living in it all together, and shifting continually with its currents.

FEEL THE STRETCH

For lasting change to occur, we have to invest ourselves — put a little "skin in the game". Therefore, from time to time, through 15 different exercises, I'll ask you to answer questions to stretch your thinking-feeling mechanisms. Take a moment to look beyond immediate or easy answers. Dig in as deep as you can, allowing yourself to move through any moments of discomfort to find your most authentic response. You may have already noticed that I frequently refer to *feelings*, so let me explain their importance in the change process. They're a huge factor in our ability to achieve desired change quickly and effectively.

As I define them, feelings and emotions are basically the same thing. (Of course, every expert will have his own definition.) But feelings and *thoughts,* on the other hand, are fundamentally different; so it's *essential* to tell them apart. Whereas thoughts generally seem to come from inside our head and mind, feelings are waves of energy, power, sensation, sensitivity, etc., that sit in or move throughout our bodies. Our behavior is built on a platform of feelings as well as thoughts. So learning to consciously and wisely harness the power of our feelings, and better understanding how our thoughts and feelings interact, can be enormously useful in the change process.

What lies behind us and what lies ahead of us are tiny matters compared to what lies within us.
Henry David Thoreau

Dig in a little; allow yourself to move through moments of discomfort to find your most authentic response.

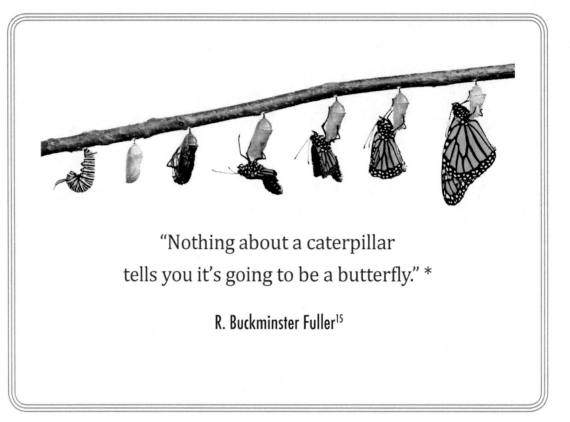

"Nothing about a caterpillar
tells you it's going to be a butterfly." *

R. Buckminster Fuller[15]

* Of all the analogies and metaphors I know for transformation, the butterfly may be the one that most frequently comes to mind.

3
GAMECHANGERS AND PREDICTORS

This short chapter introduces the fun and practical approach I offer in Embracing Change: five game-changing keys to any change or accomplishment you're considering. Each represents a major capability or way to tackle any change situation. Near the end of this chapter I'll also talk about some change *predictors* — already familiar abilities and skills that can get you quickly through the most difficult moments in achieving desired change.

Imagine the GameChangers in any configuration you want.

You'll see these GameChangers on every wining team working interactively.

You'll see these GameChangers on every wining team working interactively. Almost anything that arises in the process of change can be found within one or more of them. The order in which I present them reflects what I've found to be the easiest sequence in which to explore them, but there isn't a universally correct sequence. It's up to you to ask yourself or others questions that determine which GameChangers require attention in the process of reaching your desired change goal.

THE FIVE GAMECHANGERS

- Clarity
- Connection
- Conditions
- Motivation
- Action

The Five GameChangers will help us understand what's going on both internally and externally, and what's needed in any change situation or challenge.

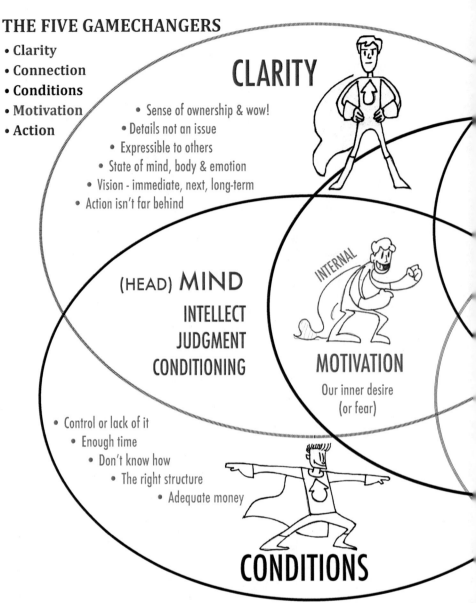

CLARITY

- Sense of ownership & wow!
- Details not an issue
- Expressible to others
- State of mind, body & emotion
- Vision - immediate, next, long-term
- Action isn't far behind

(HEAD) MIND

INTELLECT
JUDGMENT
CONDITIONING

INTERNAL

MOTIVATION

Our inner desire
(or fear)

- Control or lack of it
- Enough time
- Don't know how
- The right structure
- Adequate money

CONDITIONS

In this diagram we see The Five GameChangers with some of their key attributes and two other elements of our personality: MIND and BODY. Here, the Gamechanger, Motivation (appearing twice in a central role as both internal and external) interacts directly with the four others, though they all intersect. We want and need all five on our side working for us. These GameChangers will help us understand what's going on both internally and externally, and what's needed in any change situation or challenge. **See specifics above in light grey type.** Likewise, achieving desired change requires that

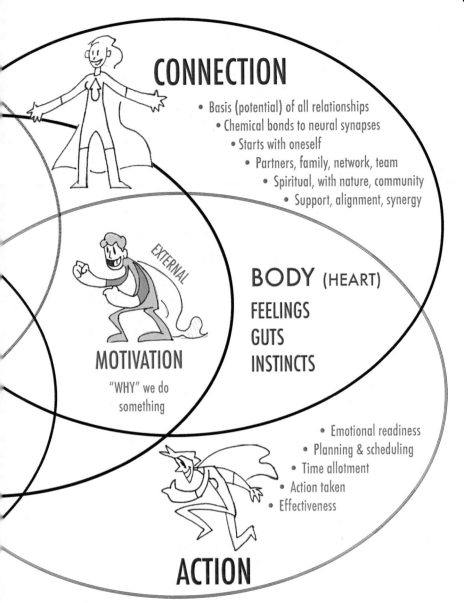

CONNECTION

- Basis (potential) of all relationships
- Chemical bonds to neural synapses
- Starts with oneself
- Partners, family, network, team
- Spiritual, with nature, community
- Support, alignment, synergy

BODY (HEART)

FEELINGS
GUTS
INSTINCTS

EXTERNAL

MOTIVATION

"WHY" we do something

- Emotional readiness
- Planning & scheduling
- Time allotment
- Action taken
- Effectiveness

ACTION

You are the captain of your own desired change, and you've been at the helm a while.

we work with all five of them in guiding both our conscious and unconscious behavior. You are the captain of your own desired change and you've been at the helm a while. You're accustomed to and comfortable with things being a certain way. But you've also probably observed that valuable signposts or landmarks are not always visible or easy to spot. There are hidden dangers or traps to fall into, which can lead to big frustration or lack of progress. Allowing the Five GameChangers to serve as your personal guides to change will accelerate your progress immeasurably.

Ideally —
presuming you
were willing
and able — you
might engage
a professional
coach or mentor
to help you with
the changes you
want to make.

RECOGNIZING PATTERNS

Using the Five GameChangers will empower you with a do-it-yourself process of self-coaching. However, you might also engage a professional coach or mentor to help you with the changes you want to make. Either way, I recommend you look for assistance from someone you respect and trust, who you think can be objective, honest and direct. This may not be easy to do, yet it's a function of almost every type of voluntary sustainable support group, from the Young Presidents Organization (YPO) or Vistage to Weight Watchers and AA — as well as any successful family or team.

If I was coaching you one-on-one, I would be asking you a lot of questions and in all likelihood diagramming your answers on a white board. Capturing the essence of your answers in words and phrases, in multiple colors, with different shapes, lines, and visual images, I would create with you a kind of map of your reality or way of seeing your situation, This would enable you to stand back and look with greater objectivity at the patterns within those conversations areas of your life you'd like to change. On this map we would be able to see the presence of these Five GameChangers as well.

Let's say you want to change a visible behavior pattern that's been difficult to change through conscious choice. Maybe, for example, it's being on edge and not more relaxed in certain interactions, like making sales calls. First, we'd want to identify — *without judgment* — how this automatic behavior pattern works and what's driving or triggering a specific pattern within the overall sales process. Using the GameChangers as your personal change dream team can make it easier to observe *what is* and move into *what could be*.

ESSENTIAL CHANGE SKILLS — THE PREDICTORS[16]

Achieving desired change doesn't usually follow a predictable straight line. It occurs over time, the result of moments when:

1) *You tell the truth faster, compassionately,* with yourself and others, to create a state of clarity, self-awareness and greater choice.

2) You cultivate a *readiness* and *desire* for change that can be ignited by some *insight or bit of clarity*, often due to a loss of some kind, like your health, a job or relationship.

3) You *lean into your discomfort* and allow yourself a degree vulnerability, to begin dissolving resistance, insecurity, inertia, etc.

4) You *get support* from others. You tend to do far better in life with belonging, connection, shared experiences and assistance.

5) You *let go* of something you're hanging onto. Executives must relinquish total control to delegate effectively. To sky dive, you have to take that one big step out of the plane. Letting go has many names: release, acceptance, forgiveness, elimination, etc. This is true for any desired movement throughout our lives — whenever we feel stuck. Letting go thus becomes one of the most useful life skills to develop.

6) You *take responsibility* for your own growth, which means owning what's in the way, like doubt, fear, shame, blame, etc.

As these essential self-change abilities and skills will move you forward faster, I4 call them *predictors*. When you practice them, your progress toward desired change is more rapid because you're not actively resisting change or perpetuating your own obstacles or a state of stuckness.

> Letting go has many names: release, acceptance, forgiveness, elimination, etc.

LETTING THINGS GO — A SUPERSTAR PREDICTOR

As you'll see throughout the book, these predictors, like the six I've listed on page 23, are super-facilitators of inner change. They're gamechanging practices that will accelerate the shift you're looking for. Let's focus for a moment on predictor #5, Letting Things Go, because it invokes two other predictors: telling the truth faster and leaning into your discomfort — being vulnerable. [17]

For our purposes vulnerability means choosing to be open and honest — at least with yourself — about your weaknesses. Increasingly, I see people relating to vulnerability as a strength that enables them to let go of things faster. Both have become popular themes in movies, too. The Oscar-winning song *Let It Go* from Disney's 2014 Oscar-winning movie *Frozen*, expresses the theme of embracing change and letting things go in epic fashion by a heroine confronting a transformational leap as she gloriously sings:

> *"Don't let them in, don't let them see*
> *Conceal, don't feel, don't let them know*
> *Well, now they know!*
>
> *Can't hold it back anymore*
> *Let it go, let it go.*

Disney has sold more downloads of this song than any in its history. Its YouTube sing-along version,[18] has almost 900,000,000 views — many by parents. While its message might seem superficial at first, letting go is too sparsely practiced given how it can accelerates desired change. A good friend of mine, an executive who coaches his son's high-school baseball team, introduced the song as way to get his players to get over their errors faster. Perhaps the most difficult category of things to let go of in life are the memories we hold onto from the past — both conscious and unconscious.

Am I actually practicing the *fundamentals* to achieve the changes I want?

4
CLARITY   (The First GameChanger)

In this chapter, we'll explore the triggers and states that generate clarity, that precious state of mind and body that to a large degree enables and compels us to get things done effectively. You know you're operating in a state of clarity when you're ready for immediate and effective action. A lack of clarity is one of the things that thwarts action. When we're not making progress toward a goal, chances are we're not yet as clear* as we need to be about it. Here's the problem: when something isn't clear, we may not want to acknowledge it. Doing so might make us uncomfortable. Clarity makes us feel in control; we know what's happening.

One thing that makes it easier to identify inadequate clarity is to ask others for their perspective. This allows you to unhook from your own point of view and see what others see. Example: Salespeople must help their prospects be clear about what they need most — and vice-versa. If the rep doesn't push for clarity, the client won't likely get what he most needs, yet clients don't like to reveal all they know. Ironically, in this case, clarity is inhibited.

Some of the questions that Clarity asks are:

1. Do you have all the information you need to act or decide? What might be missing?
2. What *exactly* is your desired end result?
3. Is the path to your desired result clear?
4. Do you know where you are on that path?
5. If you're not taking the actions you know you need to take, do you know what's in the way or stopping you? What are the obstacles you need to overcome?
6. What kind of support do you need most?

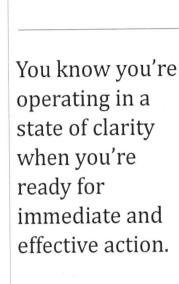

> You know you're operating in a state of clarity when you're ready for immediate and effective action.

* or, as we'll see later, possibly not as motivated, or that a critical condition isn't met

> By the time we're five, our response patterns to change have become well-established.

CLARITY AND CHANGE, THE SUPERCURRENT

To sharpen our sense of how clarity impacts the way we see (let alone embrace) the change process, let's revisit the metaphor of change as an ocean. As it moves around us from every direction, we can barely realize its enormity. We have lived in this constant, biological, sometimes calm, often-turbulent relationship with change forever. Of course it triggers strong and often negative emotion in us; we're in a kind of ongoing struggle with it for most of our lives. We dislike and fear what's unknown and things we can't control, Yet at any given moment, we can only enjoy a certain amount of clarity as to what's really going on.

Most of us have an innate need for control in our lives. In response to things we can't fully see and control, we might practice *believing* that certain things are within our control when actually they aren't. Examples: how our employees are always going to behave, or the time it's going to take us to get somewhere in our car. It takes only moments to realize we're not actually in as much control as we thought we were. From getting a job to losing one, or being without a smart phone for hours, change can elate us, or seriously mess with our sense of well being.

Psychologists tell us that by the time we're five, our response patterns to change have become well-established, though it's possible to alter these patterns. Our flexibility toward change thus forms the basis of our perspectives about our choices in life.

Getting a sense of your own change perspectives?

MEASUREMENT

One means of achieving greater clarity and winning at the change process is **measurement** — a hedge against uncertainty — what we can't see coming. Measurement tells us what we now *have* in the face of what can and will change in time — in minutes or months. Professional managers have long known that if they want to control or improve output, they have to measure it. It's critical in gaming, sports, sales, finances, marketing, manufacturing, engineering and medicine, where everything is measured or counted. Weight Watchers harnessed the powerful leverage between measurement, choice and personal performance back in the 1960s. Much of the success of Internet marketing is based on the invisible tracking and measuring of browsing behavior.

As measurement delivers clear feedback it prompts greater preparedness and anticipation. That's why accurate measurement is essential. Why wouldn't you want to establish a goal in your fitness program when you can quickly and easily plan and measure your progress along the way? Being able to see your results and modify your behavior accordingly adds clarity and certainty to the change process. So why not deputize *good* data as an expression of clarity to make it your ally and learn from the feedback it offers along the way? The enormous popularity of fitness trackers like Fitbit, Jawbone or Apple Watch, attests to the power of this practice.

Whether your desired change item is something you can measure with a device — like the number of steps you take each day, or something far less tangible — like how you feel hour by hour — the better you can identify any steps in your progress, the more effective at achieving desired change you'll become. Get some greater clarity with the exercise on the next page.

When you think about desired change, will you operate out of habit or out of possibility?

_____
_____
_____
_____
_____
_____

What will you do with the data?

_____
_____
_____
_____
_____

EXPLORATORY EXERCISE #3 – MEASUREMENT

List at least three specific ways you can measure your progress in implementing your desired change.   Example: Want to get more sleep? It means going to bed or arising earlier, or both. You can log your sleep times: Eyes closed and open, and the number of hours. You could do this X number times for three weeks.

Suggestion: The actual times you go to bed and get up, or actual sleep times – or all three.

1. _If you use some kind of homemade chart, you could also note how you feel at the end of the day_ ___

How will you collect the data?   _manually, or with devices now on the market_ ___

What will you do with it?   _share with someone, look for correction, celebration, growth_ ___

2. _____

How will you collect the data? _____

What will you do with with it? _____

3. _____

How will you collect the data? _____

What will you do with with it? _____

4. _____

How will you collect the data? _____

What will you do with with it? _____

5. _____

How will you collect the data? _____

What will you do with with it? _____

PERCEPTION → BELIEFS → BEHAVIOR → RESULTS

Here's a key change progression: *perception* triggers *belief*, which stimulates *behavior*, which leads to *results*. Let's look at this progression in some achievements of Steve Jobs,* a master practitioner when it came to altering people's perceptions. Jobs brought forth more industry game-changers, legendary product introductions and out-of-the-ordinary customer experiences than any innovator of his time. Yet often people saw what he wanted to create as crazy or impossible.[19] His perception of what was possible, like the little perfectly round rubber ball inside the original track mouse that his engineers insisted couldn't be made — ultimately altered major industries around the world.

In the post-depression Germany of 1935, the stage was set for WWII by altering the perceptions of the German people through the propaganda film, "Triumph of the Will." Most people living today have never heard of the film, but it was largely the tool that turned an otherwise civilized population into killers. Martin Luther King, Jr., the Beatles and Michael Jackson altered world's perceptions of what was possible in their reality. Public perception drove mass behavior in the panic that generated runs on banks in the Great Depression. Denial (another form of perception) of unethical lending within the banking industry lead to the global financial crisis of 2007-2008. As innovators today strive to sell their ideas and products to us, their ability to alter our perceptions is the equivalent of having a giant magic wand.

> Public perception drove mass behavior in the panic that generated runs on banks in the Great Depression.

PERCEPTION   BELIEF   BEHAVIOR   RESULT

*About six times in this book I refer to Steve Jobs, founder of Apple. Though his treatment of others, as is well documented, could be brutal, even unethical at times, he provided us with a ready source of worthwhile change-related stories.

In the game changer where David slew Goliath, the giant hardly knew what hit him.

ALTERING PERCEPTION — CHANGING THE GAME

Shifting our perception (seeing something differently) marks the starting point of desired change. Though almost anyone has the ability to change his mind, doing so isn't always easy or natural. Sometimes just realizing your true motivation — a hidden *why* — can be a gamechanger. Regardless of what we call it — greater awareness, clarity, intuition, imagination, etc. — being able to shift our own or others' perceptions is a powerful thing. A trim tab is any mechanism that effectively alters your direction. Thus shifting your perception is a trim tab for achieving desired change, which can take place over moments, days or months.

The trim tab turns the rudder, which turns the ship.

GAME CHANGING — WAY BACK

According to biblical history, David slew Goliath about 3,000 years ago when he pulled a devastating gamechanger on the unbeatable Philistine. Apparently Goliath hardly knew what hit him before it was over. He was expecting direct, hand-to-hand battle with a heavily armored soldier he easily could have killed. Instead, an unknown teenager crippled him with a surprise, lightning-fast, bull's-eye to the head with a sling-shot. It was a shift in tactics Goliath never anticipated, even though soldiers armed with slings were common in armies of the day. David acted on an unexpected possibility to change the game.[20] According to Homer, the Trojans learned a similarly large surprise lesson from the Greeks at the end of the Trojan War.

MAKING CHANGE VISUAL

The more visually engaging we can make our change process, the more effective we will be at achieving our desired change. To this end, pictures and words can work synergistically. According to a vast amount of research, "Vision is by far our most dominant sense; taking up half our brains resources."[21] Here's the basic reason: Biologically our sense of vision works almost instantaneously to activate enough emotional readiness to ensure our survival. While many pictures are worth a thousand words, the right pictures are priceless; they will move people to action.

Pictures in the form of maps, models and "dream or vision boards" can play a valuable role in your change processes, too. Visual images readily spark awareness, clarity and resolution because *what we see triggers our emotion*. When we want action, we need to give people compelling pictures, or tell them a story that evokes images vivid enough to trigger strong emotion.

Renowned TED presenter, brain researcher and author, Jill Bolte-Taylor, drives the point home: "Although many of us may think of ourselves as thinking creatures that feel, biologically we are *feeling creatures* that think."[22] Thus, when we look at the internal process that's part of achieving desired change, the more visually and emotionally engaging we can make the process, the better. As the Five GameChangers characters represent all the major elements of change, they can help us *visualize* what's needed.

> Vision is by far our most dominant sense; taking up half our brain's resources.

SEEING YOURSELF DIFFERENT*

In today's fast-changing world, success requires flexibility: the ability to see things through different eyes or points of view, to shift your perspective from the front, sides, top, bottom, inside, close-up and far away. It means appreciating things as much from others' standpoints as from your own.

We'll call this capacity perceptual flexibility,[23] and it's golden. Great leaders today seem to have this trait in a big way. We probably all have more capacity for it than we actually practice. One main point of this book is to help you develop yours.

Who do you respect or admire for demonstrating perceptual flexibility? Consider people who thought something different about themselves and what was possible and then acted on it. What might you have in common with them? Here are 10 examples of past and present world-class leaders to spark your own list:

Mahatma Gandhi, preeminent leader of Indian independence
Renata Chlumska, world explorer
Oprah Winfrey, entertainer and producer
Nelson Mandela, first black president of South Africa
Coco Channel, fashion designer
Janet Yellen, chair of the Federal Reserve
Dr. Wangari Maathai, Kenyan activist and Nobel Peace Laureate
Walt Disney, cartoonist and visionary entertainment pioneer
Jacques Cousteau, undersea diver and pioneer in oceanography
   who pioneered the first SCUBA equipment

What expanded perceptions of yourself might be a stretch for you? Will your focus be inward, outward or a balance of both?

* This is a nod to Apple's highly successful "Think different" advertising
   campaign used from 1997-2002 and mentioned on page 37.

We'll call this capacity perceptual flexibility, and it's golden.

How do you see . . .

? yourself ?

Inward or outward?

MAKING THE INVISIBLE VISIBLE

Clarity extends into the other four GameChangers as well — especially into motivation. Steve Jobs had a particularly well-developed ability to pinpoint someone's essential motivations and bottom-line his options. How he finally persuaded John Scully, the CEO of Pepsico, to become Apple's CEO in 1985 was by asking a now famous question: "Do you want to spend the rest of your life selling sugared water or do you want a chance to change the world?" Scully, of course, said yes to the latter.

sell sugared water. . .   *change the world?*

   OR

Though *Embracing Change* contains an entire GameChanger (Chapter 7) on motivation, we pause to focus on it here momentarily because we need massive clarity about it to make desired change. Motivation is the reason we do what we do, and it's often hidden, unconscious or beneath the surface, a reason or two that a situation or pattern we see unfolds in a particular way. It can be, for example, rooted in an event or a need, like for a feeling of power or control. A need for power expresses itself in the drive to create an effect regardless of what others think and feel.

The clearer you are about your own or anyone else's motivations, perceived opportunities and inner constraints (conditions), the better you can see how to help that person or yourself achieve his desired outcome. It may, however, require some insight.

> We pause to focus on it here momentarily because it's one of the first things we need to have greater clarity about.

CREATING FOCUS THROUGH PICTURES

Internal images of change can be powerful motivators. How we visualize a desired change in our mind and imagine it as good or bad, will determine how we embrace or resist it.

Neurologically, images trigger emotional connections in our nervous system. That's why we say: "A picture is worth a thousand words." We don't just *see* it; we have a *feeling* about it, too. We may not yet fully understand the science of how it happens, but we experience its power in our lives. We store a never-ending river of images in our memory. Our brains and nervous systems are emotional association networks that run 24/7 for a lifetime.

Take this famous quote from Wayne Gretzsky, probably the greatest hockey player of all time. "I skate to where the puck is going to be." In a few seconds, with 10 words, Gretzsky painted us a mental picture with enormous meaning. We see action and movement, feel the scene, hear the slap and register its meaning.

Steve Jobs was a master of whiteboard visualization, which helped him direct focus and facilitate decisions. In a famous critical strategy session with a room full of Apple product managers, he drew four lines to compose a simple "2x2" strategy. Atop the two columns he wrote "Consumer" and "Pro." He then labeled the two rows: "Desktop" and "Portable," and commanded: "We need one product in each quadrant."[24] It was a turning point for Apple, which went on to become the #1 company in the world.

> ## Images trigger emotional connections in your nervous system.

	CONSUMER	PRO
DESKTOP	MODEL 1*	MODEL 2*
PORTABLE	MODEL 3*	MODEL 4*

* To identify the specific models this story refers to would probably require an Apple historian. This might be a fun 2nd Edition feature.

EGO

Ego is an invisible but essential player in both your own makeup and the landscape of change. You've known ego for most of your life. To represent ego visually, I created a character named Edwin Codswallop,* who exists in countless forms and every personality. Though none of us has ever seen ego in physical form, we know he's armed with amazing capabilities and tendencies. Ego can be our ally or enemy. It drives us to be both efficient or clumsy, creative or destructive.

In many ways, ego is like the mother and father of our habits. As part of our mental apparatus, ego generates, uses, nourishes and protects our habits: how we eat, sleep, work, talk, sit or take a stand. You name it; ego protects it. Ego is thus a powerful function in our mind, one we're often both conscious and unconscious of as we move through life. Whenever we're pushed to look at our fears, we can count on ego to show up and do battle.

> In many ways, ego is like the mother and father of our habits.

Edwin Codswallop

Often when you're up against a challenge or opportunity, you might think your *limited self* is who or what you are. That's the protective ego saying, "You can't do that; you're not good enough." But each one of us is actually much greater than our ego. Ego is that voice inside us that says: "I'm right!" or "I'm going to have my way!" When confronted with change, it's ego who declares: "There's no way I'm going to change. That's just the way I am." Ego is convinced that *he's* the star of the show and there is no other reality for than his own.

"*Codswallop" is an English colloquialism for crap, nonsense, BS. See page 47.

> Through stories of change, courage, breakthrough and vulnerability, you can share the best of yourself.

STORYTELLING 1: CONTEXT FOR DESIRED CHANGE

Great stories about change provide clarity and perspective that involve courage, breakthrough and vulnerability. Someone inside you is the lead writer, actor and director in the story of *your* life. Since you're looking to re-direct your own main character's behavior, seeing your own story more clearly can accelerate your own desired change. By becoming more conscious of, then articulating your own stories, you may discover patterns in them, like fear or avoidance, with which you no longer want to identify and have the choice to let go. Or you may see strengths and assets you want to develop further.

As examples of transformation stories that have been capturing our imaginations since the 1940, let's consider the animated films of Disney, Pixar films and James Cameron:

PINOCCHIO becomes a real boy by being "brave, truthful and unselfish."

THE LION KING – Simba matures from timid lion cub to confident adult.

LITTLE MERMAID – Arial gets a pair of legs, finds true love and joins the human race.

FROZEN – Elsa changes from a runaway queen to a confident sorceress in a frozen castle as she lets go of her fears.

AVATAR – Jake, transformed by the Na'vi people, takes up the struggle against the Na'vi's enemies after switching his identity.

What human-acted films or other stories about change do you know of? How can these stories help you better articulate your own story line (or "arc") as it's called in the storytelling business? How might these relate to your own desired change story?

EXPLORATORY EXERCISE #4 – STORYTELLING

WHAT STORIES MIGHT YOU ADD TO THE LIST TO THE LEFT?

_____

_____

_____

_____

_____

_____

_____

WHAT DO YOU FEEL IS THE ESSENCE OF YOUR OWN LIFE STORY?

_____

_____

_____

_____

_____

_____

_____

What do you feel is the essence of your own life story?

> Being able to see things differently is critical to success.

STORYTELLING 2: KNOWING WHEN TO LET GO

Reflecting on exemplary desired change stories will provide inspiring reference points for your own transformation. To spark your own memory, here are three "getting off it and moving on" examples from Apple, courtesy of the biography, *Steve Jobs*.

Story #1. In 2001, Apple launched the first-of-its-kind Apple Stores amidst strong misgivings about the concept expressed by its own Board of Directors. Its Board Chairman, Ed Woolard, stepped down from his position rather than get into a fight with Jobs about it. The stores went on to become enormously successful. The lesson? Be ready to change your point of view.

Story #2. Late in the initial store development, one of Jobs' key team members saw a critical error in their initial store layout, an error that would necessitate a major "rewind" on the project. In a matter of hours after his initial upset over the realization, Jobs let it go and moved forward. He was often quoted as saying he valued mistakes as part of any creative process.

Story #3. When Apple released its iPhone 4 in June 2010, an episode called "Antennagate" created history when a technical flaw became a major issue in the eyes of the business media. Jobs changed the game by declaring to the public: "We are not perfect. Phones are not perfect. We all know that. But we want to make our users happy." In this bit of Apple newsmaking, getting off it made marketing history.

What stories do you know about being able to see things differently to get off it and move on faster to success?

EXPLORATORY EXERCISE #5 – OPPOSING FORCES

Stepping back to look at our Big Story themes from a distance, let's consider some basic conditions in life that can make achieving desired behavior change the challenge it is — like opposing forces within us or in our surrounding situation. Take a moment below to fill in some concrete examples of opposing forces operating in your own life.

Conscious versus unconscious _____

_____

Possibility versus what's known _____

_____

Risk and vulnerability versus safety _____

_____

Stress versus ease _____

_____

Short-term versus long-term _____

_____

Visible versus hidden _____

_____

What's said versus what's felt _____

_____

Can versus can't _____

_____

Others that come to mind _____

_____

Consider some basic conditions in life that make achieving desired behavior change a challenge.

> If you feel stuck in or disempowered by your story, at any time you can step back with a degree of objectivity and see yourself in the pattern that is recurring.

STORYTELLING 3: CORPORATE EXAMPLES – GLOVES

Consciously or unconsciously, many of us live in and repeatedly re-enact one or more of our life stories — and we do have some great ones. What does this mean? Basically, our actions are rooted in recurring themes that continue to loop in our minds. These stories emerge from old perceptions and beliefs — like fear or self judgment — which don't necessarily serve us any longer. The acronym FEAR: False Evidence Appearing Real, is useful to keep in mind here. If you find yourself predictably re-living some undesirable plot lines, repeating the same stories in different settings and circumstances or with different people, maybe it's time acknowledge it. As a skilled practitioner of change, you have more choice than you might currently realize.

Again, I'll use myself as an example. Over the course of 22 years, I was a highly productive employee in several long-term management positions. After being laid off from my full-time position in 2007, I looked back and realized I'd played out a pattern in each different job situation. I was a model employee, yet I also felt an ongoing sense of struggle in my role. I never felt my contribution was fully appreciated. The common denominator was me, of course. My feelings came from a long-standing inner story wrapped around a belief that I couldn't fully trust in my own value.

While we may be able to see our own patterns, just as easily, we may not. It's easy to function in state of denial about them when we're justifying such patterns. Sometimes we're proud of our stories; sometimes we feel ashamed. If you feel stuck in or disempowered by your story, at any time you can step back with a degree of objectivity and see yourself in the *pattern* that is recurring. Let's look at an example of how seeing a recurring behavior pattern accelerated a breakthrough in a corporate setting.

In their wonderful book *Switch: How To Change Things When Change Is Tough*, Chip and Dan Heath provide one story after another of how real people have achieved substantial changes in behavior in some remarkable ways – large and small. Each story begins with taking a step back in order to see a larger pattern. For me, their most memorable story is one called "Gloves on the Boardroom Table" from Jon Stegnor. [25]

"We had a problem with our whole purchasing process. I was convinced that a great deal of money was being wasted and would continue to be wasted into the future, and that we didn't even know how much money was being thrown away. I thought we had an opportunity to drive down purchasing costs not by 2 percent but by something in the order of $1 billion over the next five years. This would not be possible, however, unless many people, especially in top management, saw the opportunity, which for the most part they did not. To get a sense of the magnitude of the problem, I asked one of our summer students to do a small study of how much we pay for the different kinds of gloves used in our factories and how many different gloves we buy. I chose one item to keep it simple, something all the plants use and something we can all easily relate to.

> *"To get a sense of the magnitude of the problem, I asked one of our summer students to do a small study . . ."*

"When the student completed the project, she reported that our  *factories were purchasing 424 different kinds of gloves! Every factory had their own supplier and their own negotiated price. The same glove could cost $5 at one factory and $17 at another. Five dollars or even $17 may not seem like much money, but we buy a lot of gloves, and this was just one example of our purchasing prob-*

lem. . . . Even I couldn't believe how bad it was. The student was able to collect a sample of every one of the 424 gloves. She tagged each one with the price on it and the factory it was used in. Then she sorted the bags by division in the firm and type of glove.

"We gathered them all up and put them in our boardroom one day. Then we invited all the division presidents to come visit the room. What they saw was a large, expensive table, normally clean or with a few papers, now stacked high with gloves. Each of our executives stared at this display for a minute. Then each said something like, "We buy all these different kinds of gloves?" Then they walked around the table. Most, I think, were looking for the gloves that their factories were using. They could see the prices. They looked at two gloves that seemed exactly alike, yet one was marked $3.22 and the other $10.55. It's a rare event when these people don't have anything to say. But that day, they just stood with their mouths gaping. This demonstration quickly gained notoriety.

"But that day, they just stood with their mouths gaping. "

The gloves became part of a traveling road show. They went to *every division. They went to dozens of plants. Many, many people had the opportunity to look at the stacks of gloves. The road show reinforced at every level of the organization a sense of "this is how bad it is." People would say, "We must act now," which of course we did, and saved a great deal of money that could be used in much more sensible ways. Even today, people still talk about the glove story."*

Seeing the tabletop full of gloves was a "Whack!" to the senses — a reality so pressing to his company's executives they could not rationalize, avoid or justify it away. They had to act. This is an example of the GameChanger, Clarity, as a state of mind and body that leads to immediate and effective action. It also exemplifies a principle I explain a later that I call *physicality*.

Let's look at three more examples of getting out of one's usual mindset to make perceptual shifts safer and more predictable.

1) In 1999, when the Apple stores were in conceptual development, Mickey Drexler, CEO of GAP and a member of the Apple board, "gave Jobs a piece of advice: Secretly build a prototype of the store near the Apple campus, furnish it completely, and then hang out there until he felt comfortable with it. Jobs rented a vacant warehouse in Cupertino, where, every Tuesday for six months, they convened a morning brainstorming session, refining their retailing philosophy as they walked the space."[26] The point: Jobs and his team got physical with the changes as they were going. In short — they practiced. They took incremental steps to increase the likelihood of success in a safe and secure environment where they could experiment and learn by making valuable mistakes. While simulations like this may be common in premier corporations today, what is the practice for testing new and creative ideas in your workplace?

> This is an example of clarity as a state of mind and body that leads to immediate and effective action.

> What change or transformation stories live in the treasure chest of your experience and the lives of the people around you?

2) I spent six years working in an extraordinary meeting space, the ASE (Accelerated Solutions Environment), which belonged to the global consulting division of Ernst & Young. In this highly specialized meeting space, Fortune 500 teams created complex strategic plans modeled by a wide assortment of visual tools, maps and models to successfully launch major corporate initiatives. In these sessions, large teams from some of the world's leading companies immersed themselves in activities that enabled them to accomplish six to nine months' worth of conventional planning and decision-making in less than a week. GameChangers Clarity and Connection were hard at work.

3) In a multi-year process that reflects all five GameChangers, a remarkable corporate transformation story can be found in the 2003 business book, *To The Desert And Back*, about the $66 billion global empire at Unilever. "When the story opens, one of its divisions is in deep trouble — declining volume, eroding margins, critical quality problems — and is close to being sold off. The book documents five years of personal soul-searching, teamwork, company-wide learning conferences and experiential journeys resulting in remarkable top-to-bottom turnaround. The division grows by double digits and energizes Unilever's path to thrive around the globe. It's authentic and convincing proof that a revitalized business is about personal growth."[27]

What change or transformation stories live in the treasure chest of *your* experience and the lives of the people around you? What stories about change are inspiring or memorable for you?

STORYTELLING 4: OUR CAPACITY FOR DECEPTION

For at least 2,000 years, the commandment, "Thou shalt not lie." has stood against our tendency to deny, avoid or be untruthful about things that made us uncomfortable. Behold some examples in recent years of how that commandment still needs enforcing:

1. The Bernie Madoff scandal
2. Fraudulent securities trading and 2007 Wall Street meltdown
3. Decades of the tobacco industry covering up cancer
4. False reports made by the owners of the Fukushima nuclear plant before and after the largely preventable 2011 disaster[28]
5. Lance Armstrong's 10 years of lying and denial[29]
6. Being told the reason for the Iraq war was the threat of weapons of mass destruction (WMDs) in conjunction with 9/11

A top-selling residential real estate agent I know tells me that broken promises and empty threats are everyday occurrences in her industry. Dealing with it is simply a part of the job. About 2,500 years ago, in *The Art Of War*, Sun-Tzu, the great authority on military strategy and planning, wrote: "All warfare depends on deception." Ernest Hemingway, Pulitzer Prize-winning author, admonished the world to: "Develop a built-in bullshit detector." ... Need more evidence? How about an entire thoroughly researched book on the subject?

In 1985, 10 years before his book *Emotional Intelligence*, Daniel Goleman wrote *Vital Lies, Simple Truths: The Psychology of Self-Deception*, an extensive review of research on the subject of how people everywhere skew reality. "Self-deception," he notes, "is our means of psychic self-preservation, the currency of survival in which an entire society colludes ... central to our psychological existence." [30] Like it or not, distorting reality is what we humans do much of the time.

> "All warfare depends on deception."
>
> Sun-Tsu

BS AND ITS EFFECT ON US

Let's push a little further into this subject of deception. As Daniel Goleman observed, it's one in which our "entire society" participates willingly. My own fascination with the topic emerges from a lifetime of "buying" a wide variety of crap from people — including all the inner dialogue I've peddled to myself. As I'm far from alone in this practice, I think it's safe diving into it here with gusto.

As a consequence of the reflex I developed in early childhood — to be low-key in the presence of others' strong agendas — I let most of the BS I heard pass with acceptance. Over time, this cost me dearly. I think the most memorable single bit of nonsense I ever heard came from my father when I was about 10 years old. He and my mother had already been divorced for about four years and he frequently asked me to come and live with him 2,000 miles away — which I didn't want to do. I was getting ready to come home after spending an entire summer vacation with him and he was saying goodbye to me. He attempted once more to change my mind with the following assertion: "David, you're never going to become a man if you keep living with your mother." Perhaps he'd run out of kinder, gentler, more loving ways to appeal to my emotions. The point is: As adults we can and need to filter out the BS that's coming *at us*, or *from within us*. Some forms might be mild but other forms can be life diminishing. Egos (including our own) will employ almost anything to get their way.

You might want to take a breath here as we delve even further.

In the United Kingdom, when you want to tell somebody they're full of it, and you don't accept their reasons, justifications or ex-

> As adults we can and need to filter out a good deal of the BS that's coming at us, or from within us.

cuses, instead of saying "That's BS and you know it," you might just say: "Codswallop!" which means "That's nonsense. I'm not buying it." Every day, almost without end, we're bombarded by BS — from fluff and misdirection to misleading numbers and outright lies. Three famous US Presidential examples: #1) Nixon denying he had any involvement in the Watergate scandal. #2) Clinton telling the world in January 1998: "I did not have sexual relations with that woman, Miss Lewinsky."[31] #3) Bush's "Mission Accomplished" aircraft carrier speech (with banner) proclaiming we'd won the war in Iraq after 40 days.

©Robin Edgar 2013.

BS thrives across an impressive spectrum of behavior and often in full view.

Thus BS thrives across a broad spectrum of behavior, often in full view. It can take the form of corporate jargon or loosely understood lingo, hidden personal agendas, daily forgetfulness, postponement ("Let's deal with that at our next meeting"), obfuscation, tangents, bold and audacious claims, exaggeration of facts or percentages, misstatement of facts, rumor, and sidetracking. It's present in most forms of vagueness or abstraction, which can also include generality, misdirection and concealment. Politics and spin, by their very nature, are rooted in stretching or deleting the the truth, as most people know.

"The greatest sin of the age is to make the concrete abstract."
Nicholas Berdyaev, Russian Philosopher (1874 - 1948)

> The purpose of most BS is some kind of avoidance, deception or control.

One particular expression of abstraction I've used myself many times is that marvelous phrase: "Let's look at this from 20,000 feet." What an easy, confident and non-threatening colloquialism this is. How nice to feel above it all — as though there's nothing to worry about. But the 20,000 ft. invitation is tricky, for it can also mislead. I find the general purpose of BS is some kind of avoidance and deception, which usually carries negative consequences.

A simple counter-measure to the potential negative in someone's BS is the question: *How did you arrive at that?* (Or alternatively: What do you mean by that?). These questions offer leverage in the form of a ready-to-use BS filter. They can freeze or de-activate a BS projectile in mid-air. When we choose to use them, we can immediately discern and call attention to any BS that someone might be attempting to lodge in our brain. BS frequently produces fuzziness, uncertainty or a feeling of being knocked off track, versus greater clarity. What's *general* is actually *less clear,* though general is often good at triggering emotion. But without clarity there is little effective action. As a master of your own effective action, you want maximum clarity — thus minimal BS messing with your reality. Progress in making desired change is blocked or slowed when input from others (or yourself) is less-than-actionable or accurate.

Every day, as consumers of media, we're hit with hundreds of images and sound bites. These add to the countless experiences and impressions that have been forming the neural circuits in our brains and central nervous systems since infancy. We thus add images like these to our collective version of reality:

• Ads on every billboard and in every magazine that are "photoshopped" distortions of reality: while everyone seems to realize this, the general public keeps buying the commercial fiction.

• A new style of advertising that features a delightful series of scenic transformations in which one scene morphs effortlessly into a completely different scene instantly. How magical!

• As part of the daily grind in many workplaces, people are subjected to and thus live with a flow of predictable negativity, judgment and distortion of reality — as if it's normal and inevitable.

While each new BS image, fact or conversation might see harmless in itself, isn't there a hidden long-term cost to us? The more accustomed we get to being barraged by BS, the less likely we are to question it. One successful friend of mine describes our ongoing challenge as needing to raise the signal-to-noise ratio in our communication; there is far more *noise* than clear and valuable signal. We can accept it as normal or we can call each other — and ourselves — out on any BS when we see or hear it. This may seem at odds with our sense of how to get along with people. But if we want to achieve desired change in our world, acknowledging our own or another's avoidance with lightness, tact, compassion or even humor is an essential practice. Doing so builds respect in most relationships, too.

Not doing it is the elephant in the room.

©Robin Edgar 2013
David Winkelman

If we want to achieve desired change in our world, acknowledging our own or another's avoidance with lightness, tact and compassion is an essential practice.

EXPLORATORY EXERCISE #6 – LOOK-BACK

Now that we've spent some time exploring the value of good change stories, please take a minute and write down 10 changes you think have really affected you in life.

1. _____
2. _____
3. _____
4. _____
5. _____
6. _____
7. _____
8. _____
9. _____
10. _____

Then list 10 important changes you've made in the last 10 years. With all the possibilities there are, this exercise might make your head swim. Be sure to have some fun with it.

1. _____
2. _____
3. _____
4. _____
5. _____
6. _____
7. _____
8. _____
9. _____
10. _____

Be sure to have
some fun
with it.

THE POWER OF VISION

Clarity about a possibility — what people can create if they're adequately motivated — can become a powerful vision. This vision can then compel them to create audacious goals as steps to the achievement of that vision. While audacious goals may seem scary, risky or unreasonable, the power of vision, SMART Goals, effective planning and action can enable people to achieve amazing results. It was likely Steven Covey, who also observed: "What makes a great vision is that you can see it in your mind and it triggers a strong lasting feeling."[32] Here are three examples of organizational visions that express simple memorable clarity:

FEEDING AMERICA: A hunger-free America

APPLE COMPUTER: A thousand songs in your pocket.
(describing the first iPod)

NASA: "The U.S. should land a man on the moon and return him safely to the earth by the end of the decade."
(declared by President John F. Kennedy, May of 1961)

Almost everyone who Brian Chesky, co-founder of Airbnb, talked with about his company before its enormous and ever-expanding success, told him the idea would never work. The company now stands as one of the greatest-ever examples of a disruptive business change, and it's valued at over $25 billion. Chesky had no prior industry experience either, but he believed in the idea, based on his experience in the possibility. What skeptics and critics couldn't see was the gamechanger that Brian and his partner saw: people *would in fact* stay with and rent to strangers.[33]

Reputations are made by doing what others think impossible.
Do you have a vision for yourself?
Are you looking for a vision or open to one emerging?

> Reputations are made by doing what others think impossible.

MEETINGS THAT WORK

Let's focus for a few minutes on the power of meetings to create (or inhibit) desired change in organizations. When I worked in the ASE for Ernst & Young (page 48), we practiced an extraordinary methodology for accelerated and supercharged facilitation. This methodology and the unique environment in which the facilitation took place, was actually developed by a small and relatively unknown company, MG Taylor Corp., over a 25-year period. MGT turnkeyed its approach to E&Y, which in turn sold it to Capgemini in 2000. It's now being done by Capgemini and in different variations by many others worldwide.

The success of the ASE is based on the synergy of a set of essential factors, among them:

1. Support from executive management at the highest level
2. Having the right people in the room — spheres of influence
3. The highest quality environment, tools, resources and staffing
4. Facilitation methodology that was 98% predictable
5. Adequate time for getting the job done (3 long days+ a lot of behind-the-scenes prep time by the staff
6. Making as much as possible visible, thus easier to focus on, manage and move forward.

ASE sessions are nothing like the typical kind of meetings found in most companies today. They can accomplish more in one 3-day work session than most

> They can accomplish more in one three-day work session than most teams can accomplish in six months of conventional work.

teams can accomplish in six months of conventional work. One of the keys to this happening is making everything visible and visual — thereby managing the focus, insuring clarity, keeping people all on the same page and allowing for constant change without triggering a state of overwhelm. In contrast, it's generally understood today that most meetings run the risk of being disengaging and unproductive. Let's take a minute to look at why that is and what to do about it.

EXPLORATORY EXERCISE #7 – MEETINGS

Take a minute to write down below all of the reasons you can think of that meetings are generally not as productive as they could be. When done, share your notes with a person you work with. What ideas emerge from your conversation?

REASONS MEETINGS GENERALLY AREN'T PRODUCTIVE

_____

_____

_____

_____

_____

_____

_____

WHAT IDEAS EMERGE FROM THE CONVERSATION

_____

_____

_____

_____

> It's generally understood that most meetings today are can run the risk of being disengaging and unproductive.

CLARITY VERSUS BLAH-BLAH-BLAH

Real and honest emotion engages us with spontaneity, humor, confidence, authenticity or vulnerability, etc. Words by themselves don't typically do that. Instead, we hear a lot of BS coming out of people's mouths in words that are too rehearsed, judgmental, negative or reactive. When people who lead meetings ignore this bit of reality, they slip into the "blah-blah-blah" lane. They believe that what they're saying is taken as true or compelling, when it's usually not. It makes you wonder: Don't they know? When they go through the motions in this way, the value of their communication is actually lowered for everyone.

BS we perceive is probably more likely to disengage us, or make us uneasy or reactive. What happens when we use words that are too general, vague, conceptual, distorting or that delete specifics? It deadens our senses, decreases our clarity, lessens engagement and usually wastes everyone's time. When this happens for more than a few minutes, our brains say: *"This isn't real! I'm disengaging."* Then we covertly or politely leave or check out of the conversation — physically or virtually.

One of the people I had the privilege of working with at E&Y was a senior partner who could silence a room full of other consultants in seconds by cutting through any obstacles people were stuck on.* He nailed the issues, simply and quickly, and for this skill his wisdom was highly valued.

> **"It does not take many words to speak the truth."**
> Chief Joseph, Nez Pierce 1840 - 1904

> ## What happens when we use words that are too general, vague, conceptual, distorting or that delete specifics?

* Lee's few words were usually: "Okay it's time to cut the crap (BS)."

FACING MESSY AND UNCOMFORTABLE

From polite conversation to PowerPoint presentations to political correctness, we've learned to discuss *around* difficult issues using non-triggering words. We'll avoid making others uncomfortable because it's simply too risky to offend or alienate them. The cost of our caution can be truth and authenticity. So storytelling works wonderfully when you can make a point without being too direct, declarative or sounding like you know it all.

While much of the time we can make any situation sound fine with polite or abstract language, none of us actually lives in those paragraphs we speak or write. Where we *live* is in our feelings, our bodies, in the concrete and often messed-up world that's in a constant state of flux and reaction. In the real world, things are far more messy than tidy — from growing up and getting a job to raising children, developing a company, and staying healthy.

Executives, managers, supervisors and co-workers in almost every company and organization can be difficult at times — both deliberately and without even thinking about it. Sometimes arguments ensue, other times feelings simmer and stew under the surface until a boiling point is reached. For the sake of your full functionality and change mastery, developing the skills to tell others what you honestly think and feel in ways that don't offend is critical. These are the skills of great communicators and people who practice high emotional intelligence.

Leaning into discomfort provides us opportunities to look at some of our shadow issues — those that make us uneasy. Here's the message: If it's messy, it can be worthwhile. Forget what's easy for the moment. Easy will come with practice.

> These are the skills of great communicators and those who practice high emotional intelligence.

OUR PERCEPTION OF CONTROL

Our own personal weather front of behavior is continually shifting: from proactive to reactive, thoughtful to automatic, focused to distracted, etc. Our perceptual flexibility stretches accordingly. We can go through life seeing only a part of what impacts us, yet we often think, believe and live as though we're fully aware of and in control of all that affects us. As aware as we may think we are sometimes, many of us move through life without seeing our own blind spots. The result of not recognizing these can be pretty shocking at times. Example: I may think an interview went really well when in fact it didn't. It's from this vantage point that increasing self-awareness is a foundation of mastering change.

Consider the words to the song "Amazing Grace:"[34] *"I once was lost but now am found, was blind, but now I see."* From the standpoint of making change more predictable, the meaning of the words could apply to anyone who wants greater clarity about his own choices. You always have the option to ask yourself: How can I see this situation differently? Can I be more flexible in — or perhaps even change my point of view? Does it really help my situation to cling to or worry about x, y, z? What might I be missing in seeing something only from my own point of view?

Can I let go of my old point of view and move to one where I can be more flexible?

5
CONNECTION (The Second GameChanger)

This chapter gives us an opportunity to explore the impact of connection on change as relationships are essential to any success we want to achieve. Connection fuels our well being. It's the underlying force in culture. All the shared experiences, behaviors and practices that give us a sense of unity and identity occur through our connection with ourselves, others, a purpose, etc. If there's a fifth dimension, it could well be connection and relationship. The quality of any given connection reflects the way we're embracing that relationship. Is it wholehearted or less than that?

If we want to bring about desired behavior change, we must look closely at our relationships. Most successes are in some way based on the strength of a relationship, be it with a supervisor, spouse, partner, parent, mentor, teacher, friend — or a mission.

The kinds of questions that Connection asks are:

1. Who are the people you respect and trust most?

2. Do they know what kind of internal changes you want?

3. To what degree are you willing to be vulnerable, and share with them your most real and guarded thoughts or feelings?

4. Where are you currently getting the kind of support you need?

5. How connected do you feel each day to what you might call your center or your most authentic self?

6. Who or what brings out the best in you? How often do you connect with this person, thing or purpose?

7. Given how quickly things change in the world, who do you need to connect with each day, week or month in order to be at your best?

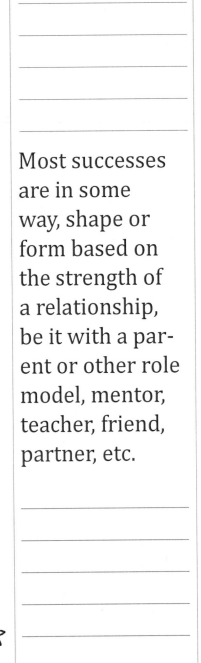

Most successes are in some way, shape or form based on the strength of a relationship, be it with a parent or other role model, mentor, teacher, friend, partner, etc.

> Connection is what humans are designed for. It is sacred, exciting, healthful, joyful, energizing, calming, etc.

CONNECTION — FOUNDATION

I began this book by saying that I hope to connect with your feelings as much as your intellect. Actually, that's *essential* for me as an author. Real connection is as much a key to successful living as any other factor, from the trillions of synapses in our brain to every relationship we will ever have. The more and varied our connections in life — with loved ones, friends, spirit, nature, energy, music, clients, employees — *and ourselves* — the more vital and alive we feel, the more productive and contributive we are, etc.

In the big picture — and this is ancient wisdom — *Connection is what humans are designed for.* It is sacred, exciting, healthful, joyful, energizing, calming, etc. I wish I had understood this earlier in life. I didn't then, but I do now. What's more, each of us can cherish, share and strengthen this sense of connection at any time, with any *conscious* breath we take. Deeply connecting with ourselves first as aware and feeling beings, is where the action begins. We can contemplate, meditate, celebrate, facilitate, even calibrate our connectedness every day.

EXPLORATORY EXERCISE #8 – WHAT COMES UP?

Here's a challenging 2-3 minutes of connection that you'll find in many personal growth disciplines, including relationship counseling, yoga and acting. Find someone you trust, or with whom you share something in common. For two minutes, stand or sit facing your partner about 24 inches from the tips of your nose, and simply look into one another's eyes without talking. If that's too much of a strain, do it for only 60 seconds. Try to avoid any unnecessary movement. Simply *be* with that person, while noticing the thoughts and feelings that emerge for you. Afterwards, take a minute and share with your partner what you felt, learned, etc. Reveal yourself.

FROM CONNECTION COMES SUPPORT

Consider three kinds of victories in life: triumph over adversity, milestone accomplishment and healing a serious illness. Each of these experiences can trigger immense gratitude and acknowledgement for those who have helped. In recognition ceremonies from the Oscars to the Olympics, from graduations to pages of acknowledgement in every book, from anniversaries to political campaigns, we see that individuals rarely get through life's big challenges by themselves. We do it with support — far better than by ourselves alone, as these three examples on video show:

A bodybuilder from Ghana trains senior citizens in NYC with love and determination, from a *New York Times* article.[35]

Arthur's Inspirational Transformation — a disabled vietnam vet, ex-paratrooper who's in horrible physical condition fights his way back.[36]

With over 19 million views, this "Power of Words" video expresses spontaneous support, a gamechanging perceptual shift, and a lesson or two for anyone. [37]

Support as a key element in desired behavior change is often missing from our daily conversation. Yet according to Michael Murphy and George Leonard in *The Life We Are Given*,[38] ongoing active peer support is the key (and usually missing ingredient) in any meaningful and effective long-term change program. Let's move into specifics that make this real.

Images from the video, "Power of Words" by Purple Plum

> Ongoing active peer support is the key (and usually the missing ingredient) in any meaningful and effective long-term change program.

> What keeps us coming back is the opportunity to be authentic, the value of being heard, felt, respected and accepted.

SUPPORT 1: GROUPS, ROLE MODELS AND MENTORS

Over many years, I've observed the essential role that support plays in success — personally and professionally — across diverse endeavors and enterprises, from sports teams to the military. I once heard Deepak Chopra tell 200 medical professionals that a doctor who failed to prescribe a medication with the clinical efficacy of support groups, which are known to extend the lives of disease survivors, might be liable for malpractice.

Such is the power of a strong support group. Currently I'm in a group comprised of eight couples that have been meeting for over 35 years. My wife and I drive two to three hours each way from San Diego to LA to be with this group. The focus of our four hours or so together is a circle of listening, in which each of us gets five minutes to "tell the truth." What keeps us coming back is the opportunity to be authentic, the value of being heard, felt, respected and accepted.

Two other connections with enormous potential to affect desired change are role models and mentors, both essential relationships in the GameChanger, Connection. Role models are valuable, either at a great distance, or up close. A mentor is a personal treasure — someone you know, respect, and trust who gives you ongoing, direct, personal feedback, assistance and encouragement. Either or both will make a difference in your career success.

EXPLORATORY EXERCISE #9 – SUPPORT EXAMPLES

Conduct your own survey over the next day or so. Ask people the question: What specific kinds of essential support have you received in life, or might have been missing in your life, on the way to your success, etc.? To make this even more useful to you, share the answers you get with someone you respect and trust, and see what emerges.

Details of such support could include: From whom the support came, relationship, what kind, what results, how often provided, over what period of time, was it volunteered or asked for, the kind of difference it made, what it was worth over time, what did it feel like, what motivated the support person to provide it, etc.

_____

_____

_____

_____

_____

_____

_____

_____

_____

_____

_____

What are the under-the-surface details of these examples?

Did any insights or aha!s emerge from these examples?

_____

_____

_____

_____

> What do Dorothy and the Tin Man, Harry Potter and Hermione, Luke and Hans all have in common besides being fictional characters?

SUPPORT 2: THE SECRET TO SUCCESS

What do Dorothy and the Tin Man, Harry Potter and Hermione, Luke and Hans all have in common besides being fictional characters? They, along with countless others, have had buddies, mentors, partners, teachers and teams who have contributed mightily to their success. Here are more well-known examples. Who else can you think of? Who's on your team and in your corner, supporting you along the way?

- Orville & Wilbur Wright, inventors of the airplane
- The Beatles: John, Paul, George and Ringo
- Rogers & Hammerstein, multiple hit Broadway composers
- Dr. Alfred Blalock and Vivien Thomas, pioneers of surgery
- Watson and Crick, the discoverers and modelers of DNA
- Rich DeVos & Jay Van Andel, co-founders of Amway in 1959

A person can develop fully and freely only when he or she is understood by another person or a group of people.

Does this image of a team that's done with professional models represent a scene you relate to or not? What would your caption be?

SUPPORT 3: KNOWING WHAT YOU NEED

We all have different and changing needs for support:
a coach,
reminder,
sounding board,
knowing glance,
sense of belonging,
laughs, hugs, or smiles,
lift up or helping hand,
wake-up call, pick-me-up,
to know we're being included,
hand-holding, technical support,
just the right person for the team,
to get a bigger picture, perspective,
solid advice, a whack upside the head,
thumbs-up, job review, acknowledgment,
that resource you need, the "I got a guy" guy,
a buddy to exercise with, to spot you under a weight,
someone who's got your back or picks you up after a fall.

Without the support of a friend, relative, peer, mentor, boss, or even a stranger, we are at risk — of not getting the feedback or assistance we need to be successful when faced with obstacles or failure. Support is the force of acceptance, love and clarity.

> Without the support of a friend, relative, peer, mentor, boss, or even a stranger, we are at risk — of not getting the feedback or assistance we need to be successful when faced with obstacles or failure.

I feel that each minute I spend with these people is a gift.

EXPLORATORY EXERCISE #10 – YOUR SUPPORT LIST

Now that you've done Exploratory Exercise #9 on page 60-61, and have saturated yourself with some positive support stories, you may see some new possibilities for yourself. Take a few minutes and begin a list with three sections. Allow it to emerge over the next few days — or keep the list going over a week or longer — forever if you like. You'll be glad you did.

Section 1: The specific **kinds of support** you want from those who can be there for you in a support role.

Section 2: Specific people in your own life who might be willing and able provide the support you need.

(To give you a feeling for what I'm describing. I offer three examples on page 67. Each minute I spend with these three people is a gift. They know who I am, what I'm about and what I'm striving for.)

Section 3: Specific kinds of support you might be able to offer others — and who you might offer it to.

1. SPECIFIC KINDS OF SUPPORT I WANT

_____

_____

_____

_____

_____

_____

_____

2. PEOPLE IN MY LIFE I COULD ASK FOR SUPPORT

_____

_____

_____

_____

_____

_____

_____

_____

3. KINDS OF SUPPORT I COULD OFFER PEOPLE IN MY LIFE

_____

_____

_____

Allow this list to emerge over the next few days — or keep it going over a week or longer — forever if you like.

SUPPORT 4: THE WAY OF VULNERABILITY

A key to getting the support you need (especially *when* you need it) is knowing the exact kind you need, then being receptive to it, then asking for it. For most of my life, I did not grasp the importance of this predictor. Instead, mistakenly, for much of my life, I thought the need for support was a sign of weakness. Boy was I wrong about that!

"The Power of Vulnerability," a 2009 TED talk that went viral, from Brené Brown, world-renowned champion of vulnerability, teacher and researcher, helped me grasp the subject and begin an active practice of it. I've watched it many times and used it in classes.[17] (http://www.ted.com/talks/brene_brown_on_vulnerability.html)

Comedian Mel Brooks described vulnerability like this:
"In the end, I've learned the audience wants the best and bravest of you. They never want you to be politically correct. They want you to be fearless, honest, crazy. They want you to do something they wouldn't do or even think of doing themselves . . ."

Needless to say, how each of us does vulnerability will be unique, and we will find the way a little easier each time with practice.

> For much of my life I thought the need for support was a sign of weakness. Boy was I wrong about that!

SUPPORT 5: EXAMPLES FROM MY OWN LIFE

• Mark, (below) is a friend with a diverse background: former professional soccer player, regional Silicon Valley shopping center manager, Body Shop franchisee and business coach. Mark shows an emotional compassion for others I've rarely seen in a man, and he fully believes that Jesus Christ is who he claimed to be. We meet regularly to talk about the state of the world; issues in our lives; and how to be more effective, present and loving.

• Tom, my yoga teacher, is a former monk whose yoga classes I've been taking almost every Saturday morning for over 15 years. In his uniquely enthusiastic way, Tom reminds us in every class that life is far more than about the have-to's, business issues and problems of the world. It's about our innermost connections, especially with the Divine. Visit Tom Kelly's web page on Facebook.

• On page 2, I related the story of how (another) Mark, an early employer of mine, provided a significant lift in life by virtually insisting that I buy a home when I was 33. He made it possible for me to pay off my old debt in less than a year in order to buy a home. His encouragement and direct assistance was invaluable; that kind of support was transformational!

I'd worked for him for only a month, yet he made it possible for me to pay off my old debt in less than a year in order to buy a home.

> "Culture eats strategy for breakfast . . ."

HOW COMPANY CULTURES CAN EMBRACE CHANGE

As you may have suspected, organizational change patterns follow much of the same tendencies we see in individuals — and why not? We move forward, stay stuck and go sideways. If we're part of a team, department or company, our ability to make collective changes pivots on our group's cultural bias toward change. For example, say that senior executives in a company decide on a strategic initiative: the transformation of that company's headquarters. Naturally, financial and market conditions will factor into the initiative's success. But just as important are that company's own internal change traditions, like creating meaningful employee buy-in along the way. Especially when it comes to massive shifts, having a strong change culture is critical to the organization's adoption of the initiative, and thus its results. Some companies are ready and geared for disruptive change and creative challenges; others aren't at all.

If you're a student of American business management, you may have heard the near legendary observation by management guru, Peter Drucker, on the role of culture in determining a company's performance. Supposedly hanging in the "War Room" of Ford Motor Corp., the famous quotation reads:

> *"Culture eats strategy for breakfast,*
> *operational excellence for lunch*
> *and everything else for dinner."*

I believe most businesspeople will acknowledge some truth to this statement. What makes culture so powerful is that there's no quick and easy way to build it or measure it. It evolves over time as a slow-moving cyclone of shared emotion, actions, beliefs, perceptions, practices, habits, leadership, traditions, environments, structures, policies and artifacts. Strong cultures seem to push people in two directions: either positively to achieve growth and empower people, or negatively to stay the same and inhibit people. How cultures manage, support and encourage change varies enormously. Here's an indicator: If culture is given lip-service as a hard-to-define, touchy-feely mascot raised by HR, it's likely that a culture will not be geared for change.

Exemplars of progressive unifying organizational cultures fill the pages of *Fast Company* magazine. Favorites of mine include the obvious picks, Apple and Google. Others include Steelcase, VF Corp and Chobani Yogurt, who's founder, in a wonderful surprise move, awarded 10% of the company ownership to it's employees. (http://www.nytimes.com/2016/04/27/business/a-windfall-for-chobani-employees-stakes-in-the-company.html?_r=0) Such cultures, in which employees, management, shareholder and customer interests thrive together, are geared and ready for change. You can quickly see it, for example in the flow of open and frequent connection between people. Is there a sense of ease and cooperation in normal conversation, or do you feel tension and aggravation? The more clearly we grasp how a culture's approach to change affects day-to-day individual and group behavior, the more effectively we can enhance a culture's collective flexibility and evolutionary skill. Culture is a collective expression of the Five GameChangers: Clarity, Connection, Conditions, Motivation and Action.

> Culture is a collective expression of the GameChangers:
> - Clarity
> - Connection
> - Conditions
> - Motivation
> - Action

At its best, a culture might even help create peak experience or a state of "flow"[39] — in which people are at their best while completely immersed in a challenge, considered by many to be our most productive state. Too predictably, however, company cultures can end up creating limiting beliefs like: *The way things are is the way they're supposed to be.*[40] — as highlighted in an article on corporate culture in Steelcase's 360° Magazine. This belief tends to kill possibility. As most of us know intuitively — we can do far better.

> Sometimes we need to say: "Stop talking; listen and acknowledge what you hear me saying."

DO WE WANT CONNECTION OR COMMUNICATION?

Generally speaking, I find only a small portion of what we call *communication* actually gets through to our heart or our guts and makes a difference. Connection, however, is truly effective or impactful communication: the *exchange of something meaningful or an authentic response*. It can happen in a split second, too — in a glance, a gesture or a moment when we don't even say anything, or can allow for laughter. Connection creates relationships of respect, trust and fun, and makes almost most other kind of communication seem like noise — or BS. Connection is what we most want and are always hungry for.

Long conversations or presentations (meetings) with little to no connection can be tortuous. The request: "Get to the bottom line." or the question, "Why didn't you say that earlier?" reflects our need to connect with each other's real meaning all the time.

When we grasp the distinction between connection (which is memorable) and communication (which often is not), desired results show up faster. In building trust, dialog — two-way exchange — beats one-way communication all the time. Sometimes we need to say: "Stop talking; listen and acknowledge what I'm saying." That isn't easy to do when there's a risk of not being heard or feeling invalidated. Without the ability to "speak up" honestly we limit our connectedness. What can you do differently starting today to create more frequent and meaningful connection?

6
CONDITIONS   (The Third GameChanger)

Our sixth chapter explores internal and external structures like the physical or social environment, which impact what we can accomplish. Sometimes these conditions are invisible to the eye, though we can often feel or sense them. Why is it essential to articulate, understand and resolve conditions? Because they reflect DANGER, LIMITATION or OPPORTUNITY. The role and impact of conditions can't really be overstated. Clarity and connection are two of the most important conditions we know.

The kinds of questions that Conditions asks are:

1. To what degree are you in emotional, financial, etc. survival?
2. Who's lifting you up or pulling you down each day?
3. What conditions do you believe are most limiting you — internally and externally? These could be things like lack of resources, time, patience, confidence, direction, structure, know-how, support, environment, peer pressure, etc.
4. Do you know exactly what the ideal conditions are for you to operate at your best?
5. When you think of the people you're most dependent on — your partner, boss, subordinates, neighbors, customers, etc., what conditions would *they* likely want to see improved?
6. Having the right "why" or motivation is a critically important condition. Do you know what your most real "why" is? (You may have many.)
7. What conditions most empower, inspire you?
8. When you assess the conditions around you that could make for peak performance, or the lack of it, would others agree with your assessment?

> We need to pay attention to and articulate conditions because they can spell DANGER, LIMITATION or OPPORTUNITY.

> What's driving many situations is often a kind of dominating emotion or thought pattern. This is what needs to be made explicit.

OPERATING CONDITIONS — KEY VARIABLES

Consider a specific change you'd like to see in your own workplace conditions. How about fewer and shorter meetings? Implementing such a change will begin with some basic problem-solving. After looking at the obvious symptoms, you'll need to assess the underlying reasons for the way things are — what I call *prevailing* or operating conditions. There will, for example, likely be at least one personal agenda being played out behind the scenes and under the surface. Prevailing conditions are not the ever-changing day-to-day circumstances that everyone knows about. The prevailing conditions I'm highlighting here are long-term *patterns*. Does the owner do regular maintenance? Does the patient normally eat healthy food? Does this team engage in a daily huddle? Does "survival" seem to be a constant issue?

We want to make distinctions between various elements of the situation, including the unexpressed emotional factors that may be driving that situation, holding it in place or not allowing it to move forward. What's driving many situations is often a kind of dominating emotion or thought pattern.[41] This needs to be made explicit, though establishing an *objective* understanding about this can be tricky. Each of us has own perspective or opinion, and things always look a particular way to us an individuals.

Whether we can physically see such operating conditions or not, we need to articulate, and if possible, measure them. They might indicate danger, weakness or threat, as in a SWOT* Analysis.[42] On the next page we'll look at four categories of operating conditions that are people-oriented and internal, versus budget or competitive landscape issues, which are more external.

*Strengths Weaknesses Opportunities Threats

1) MANAGEMENT EFFECTIVENESS: Is management mostly proactive or reactive? Are operations determined by an inspiring vision, clear goals, effective implementation — or personal agendas? When looking at any individual, team or organizational pattern, ask: What's the reason for any particular behavior? Eventually you'll get down to a very specific condition or an emotion that needs to be shifted, balanced, healed, resolved, cleared, etc.

2) MOTIVATION/PERSONAL AGENDA: This condition can often tell you what's most likely to change or not. Personal agendas constitute operating conditions of an invisible nature. Calling them out is risky, yet we need to recognize them. Many people, especially those with power and who want control, don't always want their real intentions known. Often in business we see egos can be as big a driver as any stated business or "political" agenda.

3) CAPABILITY & COMPETENCY: A truly challenging condition in business is incompetence. As documented in the book *The Peter Principle*, situations arise when individuals who are competent at certain activities are promoted to roles in management, even though they're untrained or unskilled in managing. If they're not proving themselves competent in this role, they begin to slow down or hold a department, team or even an organization hostage. It's often a complicated issue that makes life miserable for those involved when it isn't addressed effectively.

4) STRUCTURES: Systems large and small that work or don't work, environments that restrict or empower, policies that inspire or deflate morale, channels of communication and interaction that discourage or encourage the vital flow of ideas and cooperation — these are issues of structure. Too much structure limits or crushes people: not enough structure leaves them unfocused, unchallenged or inefficient. The structure has to be *right*.

> Often in business we see that egos can be as big a driver as any stated business or "political" agenda.

73

BAD NEWS? NO, GOOD NEWS

Allow me to gently offer a reference point that at first might make you uneasy. It's an invisible yet important aspect of human psychology that when better understood can be used to your advantage, rather than subjecting you to its potentially harmful effects.

Have you ever thought about the idea that negative experiences seem to be more prevalent than "good" or positive experiences? As you've no doubt experienced in life, and according to exhaustive academic research, this dominance has actually been well documented, including a 2001 research white paper, *"Bad Is Stronger than Good."* http://www.carlsonschool.umn.edu/Assets/71516.pdf

> *"Bad emotions, bad parents, and bad feedback have more impact than good ones, and bad information is processed more thoroughly than good."*

Here's an excerpt from the conclusion: *"The greater power of bad events over good ones is found in everyday events, major life events (e.g., trauma), close relationship outcomes, social network patterns, interpersonal interactions, and learning processes. Bad emotions, bad parenting, and bad feedback have more impact than good ones, and bad information is processed more readily and thoroughly than good."*

Review of General Psychology
2001, Vol. 5, No. 4, 323–370

Copyright 2001 by the Educational Publishing Foundation
1089-2680/01/$5.00 DOI: 10.1037/1089-2680.5.4.323

Bad Is Stronger Than Good

Roy F. Baumeister and Ellen Bratslavsky
Case Western Reserve University

Catrin Finkenauer
Free University of Amsterdam

Kathleen D. Vohs
Case Western Reserve University

The greater power of bad events over good ones is found in everyday events, major life events (e.g., trauma), close relationship outcomes, social network patterns, interpersonal interactions, and learning processes. Bad emotions, bad parents, and bad feedback have more impact than good ones, and bad information is processed more thoroughly than good. The self is more motivated to avoid bad self-definitions than to pursue good ones. Bad impressions and bad stereotypes are quicker to form and more resistant to disconfirmation than good ones. Various explanations such as diagnosticity and salience help explain some findings, but the greater power of bad events is still found when such variables are controlled. Hardly any exceptions (indicating greater power of good) can be found. Taken together, these findings suggest that bad is stronger than good, as a general principle across a broad range of psychological phenomena.

Centuries of literary efforts and religious thought have depicted human life in terms of a struggle between good and bad forces. At the metaphysical level, evil gods or devils are the opponents of the divine forces of creation and harmony. At the individual level, temptation and destructive instincts battle against strivings for virtue, altruism, and fulfillment. "Good" and "bad" are among the first words and concepts learned by children (and even by house pets), and most people can readily characterize almost any experience, emotion, or outcome as good or bad.

What form does this eternal conflict take in psychology? The purpose of this article is to review evidence pertaining to the general hy-

pothesis that bad is stronger than good (see also Rozin & Royzman, in press). That is, events that are negatively valenced (e.g., losing money, being abandoned by friends, and receiving criticism) will have a greater impact on the individual than positively valenced events of the same type (e.g., winning money, gaining friends, and receiving praise). This is not to say that bad will always triumph over good, spelling doom and misery for the human race. Rather, good may prevail over bad by superior force of numbers: Many good events can overcome the psychological effects of a single bad one. When equal measures of good and bad are present, however, the psychological effects of bad ones outweigh those of the good ones. This may in fact be a general principle or law of psychological phenomena, possibly reflecting the innate predispositions of the psyche or at least reflecting the almost inevitable adaptation of each individual to the exigencies of daily life.

This pattern has already been recognized in certain research domains. This is probably most true in the field of impression formation, in which the *positive–negative asymmetry effect* has been repeatedly confirmed (e.g., Anderson, 1965; Peeters & Czapinski, 1990; Skowronski & Carlston, 1989). In general, and apart from a few carefully crafted exceptions, negative information receives more processing and contrib-

Roy F. Baumeister, Ellen Bratslavsky, and Kathleen D. Vohs, Department of Psychology, Case Western Reserve University; Catrin Finkenauer, Department of Psychology, Free University of Amsterdam, Amsterdam, the Netherlands.
Ellen Bratslavsky is now at the Department of Psychology, Ohio State University.
We thank the many people who have contributed helpful comments and references. This work is dedicated to the memory of Warren.
Correspondence concerning this article should be addressed to Roy F. Baumeister or Kathleen D. Vohs, Department of Psychology, Case Western Reserve University, 10900 Euclid Avenue, Cleveland, Ohio 44106-7123. Electronic mail may be sent to either rfb2@po.cwru.edu or kdv3@po.cwru.edu.

323

How, you might ask, does this sound at all positive? Answer: It clarifies. It sheds more light on some half million or so years (give or take depending on when you start counting) of *your* human evolution. When you think about the human stress response to a perceived threat, just think: PROTECTION. That's what all our reflexes are designed to do in the presence of something we consciously or subconsciously think for a split second could be bad for us. This reflex is a protection trigger built into our deepest DNA, which long ago commanded: "Danger! Run, hide, avoid, freeze, snarl, scream, etc. — or control and dominate." As a reflex, it's automatic and operates almost every time, too. But when we can catch ourselves in a moment of reaction, we can deliberately choose a more desired behavior versus an undesired reflex.

Hindsight and lifelong learning can teach us that our automatic fight, flight or freeze responses don't always lead to ideal out-

comes. We're often better off reasoning out a situation, facing what we find uncomfortable, breathing, and working through our cycle of distress. I wish I'd realized much earlier in life how my own automatic *flight* response to discomfort, overwhelm or uncertainty became a habit of procrastination. Had I seen it, I would have saved myself a good deal of grief.

> This reflex (the human stress response) is the protection trigger built into our deepest DNA, which long ago commanded: "Danger! Run, hide, avoid, disconnect, freeze, hate, snarl, etc."

> At times we operate rationally, when it suits us, but far more often we operate by *rationalizing*.

SURVIVAL, REACTION AND EMOTIONAL HIJACKING

Survival, reaction and emotional hijacking patterns are common everyday reactive states that can be triggered at any moment. These stressful states of mind and body can stop people mid-sentence and suck the spark from them instantly or gradually over time. They can and will delay or prevent desired behavior change. Having lived a large percentage of my life in these states, thinking about them now makes me take a deep appreciative breath. Anxiety used to be a nearly continual state of mind for me that I didn't even recognize while I was living in it.

Do people really choose to be in these negative states willingly? I don't think so. I think such recurring negative states are largely unconscious patterns triggered by inaccurate perceptions and beliefs lodged in our deep mental recesses. At times we operate rationally, when it suits us, but far more often we operate by *rationalizing.* For example, in what way is chronic (and self-sabotaging) procrastination desirable or reasonable? It isn't — and I'm speaking from plenty of experience about this. It's a pattern of avoidance, which when triggered is often quickly rationalized.

Whatever our emotional patterns are, we can give names to these states in order to talk about them more objectively. This gives us the *clarity* we need to disengage faster from them as they're triggered. Observing and calling them out is the first step. In doing this we can begin to lessen their effect and control over us. The more specifically we see and name these reaction patterns when they're operating, the faster we can unhook or step out from them, and be present.

SURVIVAL is "hard-wired" in most human beings, though what I'm talking about here is emotional survival — a psychological need, not a physical one. Of course they're related. Surviving is the opposite of thriving. It's not what we call happiness, success, fulfillment, satisfaction or joy. Psychological or emotional survival means getting by: a state of relief, being okay, safe or acceptable — versus feeling like you're under siege or threatened in some way. Survival is a moment-by-moment condition, always subject to the roller coaster of situations and circumstances. Emotional or psychological survival is as pressing today as physical survival was in our earliest history. It is a baseline need we must meet in one way or another. Otherwise we feel anxious, debilitated, less-than, and we constantly have to prove ourselves in some way. On the flip side, if we get used to emotional survival for any length of time, especially early in life, we can spend the rest of our lives settling for it in some way. With such settling can come compensating behaviors that go with it, like rationalizing as a way of life. Giving up can take place over time in a thousand little ways.

> The problem is that we can get used to emotional survival and settle for it.

REACTION is a broad and readily observable category of behavior in all living things. For the most part, our reactive capacity is far greater when it comes to perceiving danger than creating satisfaction or thriving. We simply remember bad more intensely and rapidly than good (page 74). What's bad is immediately accessible; what's good is something we may need to think about. A common pattern of reaction discussed earlier is EMOTIONAL HIGHJACKING, a state some people seem to cycle in and out of much of their life. (I did, as discussed earlier.) In simple terms, it's a state when a reactive emotion runs away with us. Road rage, when acted out, provides a vivid example of this. While such moments can feel intense and uncomfortable to some, to others they can feel normal — especially when people have grown used to them from early childhood. I sometimes observe mild emotional hijackings happening in business meetings. *Do people know it when they see it?*

OBSTACLES, ROADBLOCKS, WALLS AND RUTS

Let's look at how accurately you see your own internal obstacles along the path to your desired behavior change. Some obstacles might *appear* visible and outside you, like a supervisor or situation, a lack of time or money. More often than not, however, the largest and most impactful obstacles begin with your own limiting thought patterns, which may be tougher to see.

To accelerate your desired change, you can take an inventory of such obstacles and roadblocks by asking others to help. You might even use a third-party assessment tool called a 360, which assembles an objective assessment of your personal and professional skills and weaknesses, provided by feedback from peers, direct reports and supervisors, etc. But you don't need a 360 to get useful feedback. You need only want it sincerely enough to ask for it, and then listen to the answers you get.

Then the real work begins. Think of it as scaling a wall; it's going to be difficult, so look for footholds and places to grab onto: the specifics of change — actual trigger points. Can you get creative when you catch yourself in a behavior you'd like to change? Sometimes I call myself on a behavior out loud: "Well, here I am doing this again!" It makes me laugh while exposing the pattern. Could such playful but serious self-coaching work for you? Try it!

> Think of it as scaling a wall; it's going to be difficult, so look for footholds and places to grab onto: the specifics of change — actual trigger points.

78

EXPLORATORY EXERCISE #11 – OBSTACLES

Let's look at some possible obstacles in two major categories.
Reviewing the list below, which of these are relevant to you?

EXTERNAL & VISIBLE

❒ Lack of resources (money, friends, contacts, etc)

❒ Conflict with others

❒ Shortage of time

❒ The boss won't let you

❒ No clear path seems to exist

❒ Too much conflict somewhere around you

❒ Other agendas around you

❒ Old reputations in the way

❒ Too much BS in the space

❒ Lack of support or alignment

❒ Lack of out-of-the-box thinking

❒ Other _____

INTERNAL & INVISIBLE

❒ Lack of clarity

❒ Lack of confidence

❒ Lack of know-how

❒ Confusion or ambivalence

❒ Fear or concern (any form)

❒ Lack of inner permission or self-acceptance

❒ Can't connect to purpose

❒ Can't "get out from under it"

❒ Overwhelm

❒ No clear plan or feeling of certainty

❒ No sense of control

❒ Other _____

Which ones can you begin tackling today?

Which ones
can you begin
tackling today?

EMOTIONAL INTELLIGENCE (EQ)

Whether you take a course in Emotional Intelligence, or are naturally skilled in it, a better grasp of your emotions will contribute to greater achievement. Almost all recurring *personal* issues found in workplaces today are driven by emotion. As taught by Jean Greaves and Travis Bradberry, authors of *Emotional Intelligence 2.0* and founders of Talent Smart,[43] the preeminent EQ corporate training company in the world, the four basic EQ skills are:

Self-Awareness	Self-Management
Social Awareness	Relationship Management

Harnessing the power of emotions is the most critical skill in achieving desired behavior change. That's why raising your EQ is one of the most practical things you can do — it empowers you with greater effectiveness to produce the results you want.

According to the research done by TalentSmart, the link between EQ and earnings appears so direct, every point increase in EQ adds $1,300 to an annual salary, regardless of industry, position, type of work, etc.[44]

> Almost all recurring *personal* issues found in workplaces today are driven by emotion.

JUDGMENT AND CRITICISM

EQ directly relates to judgment and criticism, so let's be clear: As social beings who live in cultures, organizations, and families, we judge, criticize,* and withhold acceptance. We do this regularly, predictably and even automatically. We do it knowingly, unknowingly, personally, professionally, publicly, and privately as an almost expected part of our social currency. As the saying goes: It's a jungle — *of judgment* — out there.

We can choose to do it far less, however. Judgment and criticism in almost any form tends to retard, rather than support desired behavior change. Judgment and criticism are negative forces that in essence suck acceptance and positive attention right out of the air. Judgment and criticism are *not* empowering; they're disempowering. Whether couched and subtle, or obvious and intentional, the result that judgment and criticism aim for is control and non-acceptance. Sometimes we need to say *enough*.

Example: In a discussion during a meeting of senior managers, it was understood that a particular process in the company was broken. I made a suggestion about a specific course of action. In an almost immediate and predictable response to my idea, a senior manager asked me if I had any data to back up my suggestion. While on one hand, this was a fair and reasonable question that he had a right to ask, he was knowingly delaying action with a rhetorical question. He already knew there was no data. It was a classic "paralysis by analysis" move, a way to avoid action. His tactical question took control of the conversation and delayed meaningful action. Judgment used in power plays like this kill countless possibilities — large and small, daily.

> Sometimes we need to say: *enough.*

* The distinction between criticism and *constructive criticism* is critical. Constructive criticism always offers a positive suggestion for improvement.

POSSIBILITY OR LIMITATION — CAN VERSUS CAN'T

The Internet is full of stories about people who've overcome major limitations to become brilliantly successful in some way. Among all the many rags to riches stories I know, Oprah's may be the best-known. She worked her way from rural poverty in Mississippi to being arguably the wealthiest, most influential and generous woman in the world.[45]

People often bust through negative external conditions when internal conditions aren't holding them back. Our challenge is to understand exactly what those inner conditions are so that any possible forms of limitation aren't holding *you* back. This distinction leads us to a second essential element as we explore working with conditions: the "can" versus "can't" voice.

When you excel in something, you're operating from possibility as opposed to limitation — *can* rather than *can't*. I call it the *"Can-Can't Toggle."* There's a voice or mechanism in your mind that talks to you, often in a limiting way. It tells you at any given moment throughout your life that you can or can't do this or that. It says to you: "I can" or "I can't". . ."you can" or "you can't." Wired to this "can-can't" toggle switch is your power and aliveness — your internal sense of what's possible and what's not. Of course, you may not always be conscious of this internal dialogue. It might be speaking in a whisper, not shouting at you. The voice isn't always right. Actually, it's often wrong when it says you can't. This has been proven countless times by breakthroughs during ropes courses,[46] athletic and artistic performances, coaching relationships, support groups, careers, therapy, etc. Each of us *can* find that power switch, and make sure it's in the *can* position most of the time.

> Of course, you may not always be conscious of this internal dialogue.

LEVERAGE = POWER!

If you want to accomplish great things, have more influence, make more money or just make a bigger difference, you need help: *leverage* — as much of it as you can get or create. This applies as much to janitors as it does CEOs, doctors, employees, supervisors, suppliers or parents. The law of reciprocity abundantly demonstrates that if you're able to help others achieve their dreams, they may be willing to help you. Achieving desired behavior change suggests leverage because there are always obstacles to overcome and we need as much help as we can get.

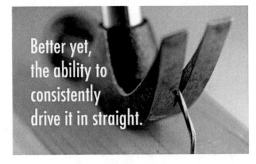

Better yet, the ability to consistently drive it in straight.

Leverage is any labor-saving mechanism that saves you time, delivers a desired result and makes your work easier. It can come in countless forms: key connections, other people's money, a bigger computer screen, networking (with the right people), having the information you need when you want it, etc. Leverage makes you stronger, faster, better, smarter and reduces the risk of not accomplishing what's essential. Other examples (in case you wanted a few more): emotional support like honest feedback from a friend or mentor, having a system or methodology that's proven to save you time, great directions or instructions. Leverage means having the best tool or person for the job, or the skill or credential when you need it.

Good marketing leverages memorable hooks, tag lines, popular celebrity endorsements, and news stories that put your launch on the news and send it viral. In building relationships, leverage grows through long-term loyalty, organically in countless

> Leverage is any labor-saving mechanism that saves you time, delivers a desired result and makes your work easier.

thoughtful and respectful moments, in the unexpected rewards and recognitions rather than formalized reviews, and in offering support.

Hamdi Ulukaya, founder of Chobani, handed over to his employees stock worth around 10 percent of the company when it is sold or goes public. 4/26/16   Photo: Alexandra Hootnick for The New York Times

> The least costly form of leverage in my view will always be great relationships.

The least costly form of leverage in my view will always be great relationships, as illustrated in the photo above. Here's a great example of a solid relationship unexpectedly turning into money for employees in a notable corporate culture at Chobani Yogurt.

Given how essential leverage is to success, what's surprising is how few people seem to aim for greater leverage in solving their problems. Whenever I go into a company to work with its people, I ask anyone I'm talking with: "Where do you get your most and least amount of leverage?" In many cases, the initial response I get is a blank look. People simply aren't thinking along these lines. Once I explain the principle and how it might apply to them, it makes sense; then the conversation is fully underway.

In achieving desired change, leverage in any form you can find is key: SMART Goals, greater objectivity, better structure, more efficient method, support from someone you trust and respect when you need it most.

EXPLORATORY EXERCISE #12 – LEVERAGE

Make a list of specific kinds of leverage you need to be more successful or fulfilled. You might start with tasks you do that are critical or repetitive, ones you like doing least (or most), those you'd like to hand-off to someone else, or that take the longest, incur the most frustration, involve uncertainty or most number of variables. Leverage saves time, money, headaches and increases speed-to-desired-results. You can also look at more general categories in life: Work, delegation, management, health practices, household chores, etc.

1. FORMS OF LEVERAGE THAT WILL MAKE A DIFFERENCE

(Also include a note or two about how you'll put that form of leverage into place. What will it take?

_____

_____

_____

_____

_____

_____

_____

_____

_____

_____

_____

_____

_____

How will you put that form of leverage into place? What will it take?

_____

_____

_____

_____

> The ASE, the Knowhere Store® and Navigation Centers® fixed a new reference point in my way of thinking and doing.

THE ENVIRONMENT FACTOR

The many environments you work, play and live in give you far more than you probably think about. In addition to location, architecture, space, light, art, color and sound, they also provide context, purpose, a sense of belonging, culture, population, movement, air quality, smell, furniture, social interaction, and functionality.

For five years I worked in three MG Taylor Corp. environments: The aforementioned ASE, the Knowhere Store® and two different Navigation Centers.® My experiences fixed a new reference point in my way of thinking and doing. What took place in these spaces, generally in a three-day workshop format, was a combination of teaching, learning, problem-solving, strategic planning and team-building.

Our clients were largely teams of 40 to 80 executives, managers, and influencers from Fortune 500 companies or larger, charged with laying out a major strategic plan for their company. The corporate teams that used these creative spaces moved through mountains of data and what-if scenarios as billion dollar initiatives were systematically examined over a

three-day DesignShop,® as they were called.

Our promise to the client was that its team would produce six to nine months' worth of normal business output in three days, along with the buy-in needed for the success of the initiative.

What those years taught me is that carefully designed environments can deliver far greater performance than in workplaces where highest possible functionality is assumed and so never considered, let alone designed into the space. "Everything speaks!" was our call to arms. It meant every little and big thing you see delivers a message about its purpose and function.

But the reverse of this possibility can be just as true. In the long run, not investing time into resourcing and outfitting an environment for what you need accomplished can be more costly than you think. As researcher Winifred Gallagher[47] points out in *The Power Of Place*: *"Settings can be more important determinants of behavior than personality."* In short, what we do or don't do with our environments, will, over time, contribute to the overall success or failure of our enterprises and communities.

"Settings can be more important determinants of behavior than personality."

THE READINESS FACTOR

Getting ready for self-change challenges us to press through discomfort and determine readiness. But it's tricky. This is where rehearsals, dry-runs, role playing, tests, measurement and critiques come into play. We need to see how people are likely to perform under pressure. Have they integrated the learning or let go of what's old and unwanted to bring in the desired behavior change?

Readiness is something you work towards over a period of time, then one day, you seem to be there! Something has shifted; you've crossed the line and feel ready — or the day has come when you must be. However, as we've seen and discussed, people will sometimes say they're ready when they're not, or that they've changed when they haven't.

> I *could be* on time if I wanted, but unless I "set it up" to run ahead of schedule, I'd probably fall behind.

Example: For many years I struggled with being on time. I used to tell myself I could be on time when I wanted to be. In truth, I was prompt about 90 percent of the time, though I often felt like I was running late. One day I realized that being on time without any struggle required a decision. I *could be* on time if I wanted to, but unless I set it up to run ahead of schedule, I would likely fall behind. The question was: Would I be early or allow my near-compulsive need to just "do one-more thing," rule the day?

Readiness is thus sometimes like a dance, in which you're not sure yet who's going to take the lead — you or your partner — your conscious or unconscious motivation? Which one will dominate? Remember Executive Function? At any point in time, we can call on him or her.

PRACTICE, DISCIPLINE AND SELF-CONTROL

"Just do it." "Practice 'til it hurts." "Wipe on, wipe off." "No pain, no gain." We've all heard expressions like these referring to the dedicated effort it takes to succeed. They suggest that growth and desired change almost *demand* we work our way through discomfort. But who can predict how many moments of discomfort there will be or just *how* uncomfortable those moments will be? This is why we can't take adequate motivation and self-control for granted — because temptation, resistance and inertia can defeat us. So steadfast practice and external support are *critical*. We need these positive forces to pull us through the difficulty of practice and our tendency to avoid the uncomfortable. Without them, we're likely to fade or give up over the long haul.

There's often more to successful individual practice than meets the eye. Critical details about successful practice aren't always obvious. The specific conditions for substantial and high quality practice, as with good coaching, the right equipment or without restrictions, can present an opportunity for greater success and provide a huge advantage. Conditions for rigorous or extensive practice, whether it's deliberate — aimed at a particular goal or generic practice, supervised by an expert, done in an ideal

But who can predict how many moments of discomfort there will be or just how uncomfortable those moments will be?

"The merit of all things lies in their difficulty."
Alexandre Dumas, author of The Three Musketeers

DISCIPLINE DISCOMFORT CONDITIONS

What are the specifics of the most difficult practice related to your own change item?

environment by oneself or alongside others — are factors that researcher-author Malcolm Gladwell, observes in *Outliers: The Story of Success*. His research reveals how the "best of the best" came to be so successful — from big athletes to John D. Rockefeller, Bill Gates and the Beatles. Factors like the quality and quantity of practice we engage in, how specifically it expands our skills, who we're doing it with and what's going on around us (to name but a few), determine the effectiveness of a practice in a huge way — regardless of the level of mastery we aspire to.

I recently hit a fitness milestone: doing 330 abdominal crunches without stopping. Pushing myself gently it took me about eight months to get there; I started at 25, when just doing 30 was painful. I might have arrived there faster, had more fun and hit other milestones as well if I'd worked with a trainer or done it in a fitness class on a regular basis. As MBA students, for example, work their way through a two-year program, they often do so in small study groups that are pivotal to their productivity and class cohesion. When such challenges, learning and goals become experiences shared with others, and we know where our investment is leading, our practice becomes far more enjoyable and effective.

While each situation requires its own set of practices, certain patterns emerge. I've had the privilege of talking with two billionaires in my life.* One was a real-estate pioneer, Walter Schneider, who co-founded RE/MAX in Canada. In a brief one-on-one conversation I had with Walter, I asked him: "Given all the factors that contributed to your success, what is the single most important one?" He looked at me calmly and without hesitation replied, "*Discipline.*" I've always remembered how clear he was about it.

What's the most difficult practice related to your change item?

* The other was a commercial real estate developer who demonstrated the immense contribution of a mentor to someone close to me.

MAGIC IN THE MIX

What we've seen in our short exploration of conditions is the need to factor in a mix of conditions when managing self-change expectations and outcomes. Whether these conditions are immediately visible, tangible, quantifiable or not — we need to identify them very specifically. The central question is: What are the conditions that support, enable or limit our success in making the change we're seeking? What matters most is how honestly, thoroughly and accurately we answer these questions.

If, for example, we're attempting to get another person to see a situation differently, the first condition is whether the other person is even listening or open to our point of view. Does he or she acknowledge our way of seeing the situation?

Examples of change conditions in companies:

What long-standing structures or traditions are in place?
Do we have the necessary information or directions?
To what degree have we objectively verified our clarity?
Have things been clearly documented, updated and distributed?
Do we have the physical, financial and intellectual resources?
Have the skills necessary to accomplish this been demonstrated?
What's the time frame under which we're operating?
Do you have clear permission, alignment, buy-in and readiness?
Are all stakeholders adequately informed? How do we know?
Was there discussion that surfaced any issues, confusion, etc.?
Is it in the budget? Has the amount been allocated?
Are people fully aware of what you've done thus far?
What's the weather going to be?
Is there trust, alignment, respect and free-flowing communication?
What's the prevailing mood, morale or understanding?

> The lead question is: What are the conditions that support, enable or limit our success at change?"

SYNERGY — THE IDEAL CONDITION

You've likely heard the word synergy, but have you ever experienced it? Imagine two or more people relating to each other with so much respect, trust and alignment that their working together as partners or a team achieves more than they initially believed possible? In a nutshell, that's what synergy is.

As shown in the unusual 2004 HBO docudrama, "Something The Lord Made," Dr. Alfred Blalock and his assistant, Vivien Thomas, who wasn't even a doctor, formed a working relationship that lasted more than 30 years. Together, they developed a shunting technique to bypass the aorta that directly saved thousands of lives. It marked the start of the modern era of cardiac surgery as the first successful surgery on the human heart in modern medicine. http://en.wikipedia.org/wiki/Something_the_Lord_Made

Synergy describes an extraordinary condition resulting from a special alignment of values, goals and personalities. It includes a commitment and willingness to do what it takes to succeed, and a lack of ego that has to dominate all the time. While talent is critical, it can show up in unexpected ways, as was seen in the "miraculous" winning men's 1980 U.S. Olympic hockey team.

> Synergy describes an extraordinary condition resulting from a special alignment of values, goals and personalities.

7
MOTIVATION   (The Fourth GameChanger)

In this short chapter we dive into Motivation, the fourth of the GameChangers, and the umbrella term that encompasses desire, intention, need, drive, purpose, vision, and identity. In short, it's the fuel for doing what we do — a combination of the why, the force and reason behind our action. We often have multiple conscious and subconscious intentions, too. Major research[48] about what does and doesn't motivate us — like incentives and rewards — might even surprise you: Traditional and obvious "if-then" rewards and consequences *aren't always at work*. Though motivation is our driver, all the words we have for it only add up to an approximation of the feeling or experience itself. In fact, our own internal experience — of a flow state or peak performance for example — may not be readily or easily expressed in words.

Motivation is a dynamic, emotional, and intellectual stew of stories, internal pictures, experiences, feelings and associations. In one respect, feeling a specific emotional state *is* our motivation. Therefore, what we want to pay even more attention to than our words for motivation is the strength of our feelings about it.

The kinds of questions that Motivation asks are:
1. What motivates your behavior or action when you're winning or feeling best about yourself?
2. What drives the behavior in you which, at least on the surface, doesn't support your winning?
3. In your experience, what motivates you most?
4. How would your team members or best friends answer that question?
5. What are the hidden motivations or personal agendas you see or feel operating in your own work environment?

What do you think motivates you most? How would your team members or best friends answer that question?

This list is only a thin slice of what's possible, of course.

EXPLORATORY EXERCISE #13 – YOUR OWN CHANGE

Remember the list below from page 8? It's placed here again, because if you've read this far and you haven't yet taken any interactive step in reaching for what you want, now would be a great time to look at what's stopping you — where you might be playing a little trick with yourself or hedging in some way.

Again, if one of these items doesn't nail it for you, create your own. This is *your* choice — something for you as an individual or as a member of a team or family. Take your time. Notice your feelings.

What I feel most motivated to change is:

Be more effective?
Get a new job?
Get to my ideal weight?
Create a loving relationship?
Resolve an issue?
Forgive someone?
Make more money?
Change or end a bad habit?
Start a positive habit?
Stop procrastinating?
Be less reactive?
Relax more?
Start doing yoga?
Have more free time?
Let a whole lot of stuff go?
Develop greater focus?
Feel more confident?
Have more time for myself?

Eat healthier?
Get more exercise?
Use intuition more?
Express greater creativity?
Move forward faster?
Make more rapid progress?
Express the real me?
Be more positive?
Be happier?
Be more assertive?
Be more present?
Be more outgoing?
Increase my income?
Feel my feelings more?
Be a better public speaker?
Identify my vision or purpose?
Make new friends?
Transform _____ in my life?

READY . . . SET . . . GO! FIND THE MOTIVATOR

Most behavior starts with motivation. Think for a moment about any programmed entertainment you might enjoy — whatever it may be — reality TV, comedies, drama or game shows. At some point what emerges is the motivation behind the performances. Whether they're successes or failures, we want to know why people do (or don't do) certain things — what's driving their behavior. Something invisible on the inside is expressing itself on the outside. When you think of any mentors or role models in your own life and the kind of success you see in them, can you bring to mind what *their* motivators were?

Motivation fuels aliveness. It's the source of your drive to do or not do something. It can be the fear of the penalty of failure or the possibility for huge recognition. It can bowl others over when it's high enough, or leave you feeling worthless when you can't find it in yourself. Once you understand your own intrinsic motivation, you will see a desired behavior change as either adequately or inadequately motivated. Certain triggers turn it on. Other triggers turn it off. When you're not on track, your dominant motivation is probably hidden, unconscious or masked.

Here's the question: Are you moving *toward* one thing — or *avoiding* another? Motivation is a core issue when identifying why we're not achieving real self-change. Now let's see how motivation is related to perception and action.

> Once you understand your own intrinsic motivation, you will see a desired behavior change as either adequately or inadequately motivated.

THE WELL AND OUR IDENTITY

Possibility, purpose and vision suggest an ancient and powerful metaphor: the *Well* — a place, source or experience inside or outside you from which you can draw life-giving meaning and inspiration *everyday* — especially in the presence of stress, fight, flight or freeze, and constant change. The *Well* (or any word that might work better for you) can help you instantly see and feel the treasure life has to offer that gets buried under your "have-to's." Having the *Well* and knowing how to quickly access it makes it easy to draw from, and then expand it by sharing it.

I associate the *Well* with the words: Who You Are — your authentic self that is connected to something greater. You can draw from or connect with this source in an unlimited way. You might even relate the *Well* to the famous line from *Star Wars*: "May the force be with you!" The influence of the force is lasting. You get this ongoing sense of larger and stronger self from having your *Well* be a place, group or reference point that's bigger than you as an individual — perhaps a cause or mission. We're talking about the power of identification here. Identity can be so strong people will fight when it's challenged or threatened.

We see this across the human spectrum, from sports to politics to religion, to your own ego. When you *don't* have something powerful and positive to identify with, you might even feel like

What does YOUR Well look like?

you're missing something in your life. Indeed you might be. What is *your Well* and where are you looking for it? At the end of your life, when people are talking about who you (really) were — your true nature — what will they say?

> We're talking about the power of identification.

POWER AND CONTROL

Human beings are generators of power. We generate all kinds of energy — physical, emotional, financial, social, sexual, creative — with which to control and manage our world, inside and outside ourselves. In countless forms we wrestle for this power. We call it influence, status, persuasion, strategy, domination, surviving, winning, etc., and we have built-in radar for sensing when power is in play. That's when, in countless discussions and arguments, we feel our emotional buttons pushed. It's when we're subject to those split-second hijackings, when we can lose our focus or sense of well being — or run off the rails. When we raise our voice, we're probably losing the argument, too, though we might not realize it. In the moments after I get angry, I always end up seeing it as my own loss of control.

When the usual "power plays" don't work — when you lose a job, a client, someone's trust, or even an argument, you might get upset or experience a crisis. Then you see the kinds of ego patterns that reflect your need for *control*. Recognizing the many ego personas inside you can give you freedom to choose less automatic patterns. Try giving them amusing names. One of the one's I'm still working on is a pattern I call Comfy. (not shown)

> When we raise our voice, we're probably losing the argument, too, though we might not realize it. Moments after I've gotten angry, I always see it as my own loss of control.

Smarty · Jerry · Boss · Wendy · Edwin · Sneak · Slyde

97

RISKING — VULNERABILITY AND COURAGE

One unusual example of vulnerability you can watch online is a 90-second segment of "Dancing With the Stars," a show my wife enjoys. In it, celebrity model, Nyle, performs a dance with his professional partner, Pita, to Simon & Garfunkel's classic, "The Sound of Silence."[49] What makes it so memorable is that *Nyle is totally deaf*, so their trust in each other is palpable and almost impossible to fake. Seeing them dance together expanded my sense of what's possible when people are fully open and in sync.

Stories of human triumph with zero Hollywood glitz, however, are abundant throughout the Internet. A short YouTube video documenting the remarkable transformation of Arthur Boorman, a disabled veteran, is always moving to see.[50] Here are two photos of Arthur — before and after his stunning transformation.

> The remarkable transformation of Arthur Boorman, a disabled veteran, is always moving to see.

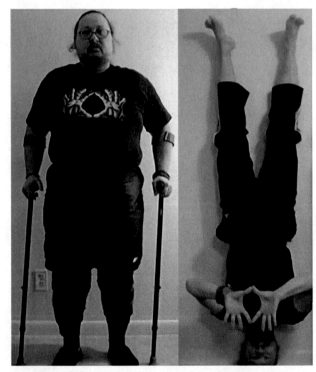

Before and after Arthur's Inspirational Transformation (with permission.)
https://www.youtube.com/watch?v=qX9FSZJu448

Arthur's story exemplifies one of the main tenants of this book: the power of and our need for support. His transformation was built on a bedrock of support from his yoga and fitness trainer, Dallas Diamond Page (DDP). Such stories can spark inspiration and reveal the emotions that motivate people to do the extraordinary. People can operate outside of their comfort zone, take risks and be guided by their heart instead of their head. The key, says Brené Brown, is to embrace the state of vulnerability with whole-heartedness,[51] starting with those you totally trust.

A powerful question you can ask yourself is this: What is it within me that will trigger my readiness and courage to face any obstacles to my goal? (You actually might want to ask it twice.)

Countless stories of individuals and teams achieving greatness by putting their comfort aside and playing from the heart, fill books, magazines, blogs and movies. Which stories do you carry within you and share with others to fuel your own fire?

> *"Our finest moments are most likely to occur when we are feeling deeply uncomfortable, unhappy, or unfulfilled. For it is only in such moments, propelled by our discomfort, that we are likely to step out of our ruts and start searching for different ways or truer answers."*
>
> M. Scott Peck
> Psychiatrist & author (1936-2005),
> *The Road Less Traveled*

Which stories do you carry within you and share with others to fuel your own fire?

AVOIDANCE BRAIN

As previously discussed, our brains developed over hundreds of thousands of years to ensure survival in a hostile environment. This ability to protect ourselves from danger enabled us to escape or fight effectively when danger in any form approached — like a threatening beast or a menacing tribe. Our *fight, flight and freeze* patterns, when triggered, are still alive and working.

For a moment, let's place all our perceived-danger-escaping patterns into a bucket called avoidance. This bucket helps us feel at least a momentary sense of escape or relief from discomfort or threat. A million years ago avoidance brain enabled us to survive a life-threatening danger. Today, as civilized beings, with so many choices available to us, avoidance is more of a tempting option.

Current-day avoidance, however, may not work out well in the long run — be it in minutes, days or months — especially when it's avoidance of some pain that's better to deal with in the present. Let's look at some examples of *avoidance brain*: avoiding the pain of exercise, the delay of gratification, facing an illness before it becomes too late, the pain of embarrassment when we need to apologize or acknowledge an error, paying a bill before it hurts our credit score. How we accept if not embrace such moments of discomfort can mean the difference between minor short-term discomfort and larger long-term pain.

Before we move onto the next chapter, ACTION, I invite you to watch an unusual TED talk delivered by Mel Robbins.[52] With great humor, she talks about generating the necessary physical force that behavioral scientists call "activation energy" required to change behavior and get through the state of "I don't feel like it." . . . Perhaps it will be a worthwhile the watch — at least once.

Let's look at some examples of avoidance brain.

8
ACTION   (The Fifth GameChanger)

This chapter on Action is about getting desired results through implementation and follow-through. When Kathy and Jerry took action in Chapter two, lives were changed. Action as the last of the Five GameChangers implies the word *effective* — thus effective enough to deliver desired outcomes — or at least the wisdom to do so the next time.* Effective action focuses on completion — not just effort, activity or being busy. Failing to do so tells you something is "off track" or missing in one or more of the other GameChangers.

THE GIFT OF FOLLOW-UP

According to Marshall Goldsmith, bestselling author and executive coach, following up with others is the #1 difference maker in the change process. Following up is how you . . .

1) Measure your progress.
2) Remind people that you're making a change
3) Imprint your efforts on your colleagues' minds.
4) Erase your coworkers' skepticism that you can change.
5) Show yourself and others that getting better is an ongoing process, not a temporary religious conversion.

The kinds of questions that ACTION asks are:

1. Do you have clarity about your outcome? Do you feel ready?
2. Is there enough time to get it done?
3. Have you adequately planned for each step?
4. Have you made the necessary connections with others?
5. Do you have the required resources and tools, etc.?
6. When will you begin? What's preventing you from starting?

Effective action, therefore, focuses on completion — not just effort, activity or being busy.

* "Action turns knowledge into wisdom." admonishes my friend, Marguerite, a highly respected fiduciary and expert in estate administration.

> As an invisible and powerful presence we seldom discuss, ego is often the biggest elephant in the room.

VOICES IN THE HEAD

Our internal dialog[53] strongly influences our behavior, so mastering it can be a key to achieving desired change. The practice we'll focus on here is getting out of our own head — a condition we've come to live with over a long time that no one else in our life actually sees or hears. Think about *that* for a moment.

If your internal conversation is positive and encouraging, your internal voice is working *for* you. If it's negative, you might want to change it soon. Certain words or phrases can operate as obstacles to actualization — or like sludge in your pipes. They're disempowering and soul-sapping, rather than nurturing. Which kind do you want triggering your actions? As Mel Robbins reminds us: "If you're in your head, you're behind enemy lines."

As noted earlier, a lack of effective action can tell us that something is *off* with the other GameChangers. Here, we interact with the GameChanger, Motivation, to find hidden sources of our negative or limiting thoughts. That source could well be ego, the invisible and powerful presence we seldom discuss. It's often the biggest elephant in the room. Ego operates through our sense of identity: we often think, believe, feel and act as though we *ARE* our ego. It's a crock! To think that we are inseparable from ego's thoughts, that we have no control over them, or have no choice other than to think and believe that such thoughts are true, is simply wrong. Insofar as we all talk to ourselves anyway, it would be helpful to talk to each other other *about* our own self talk!

TALKING BACK TO THOSE VOICES

Countless books, courses and practices show us that to some degree, as a developed skill, human beings *are* capable of controlling their thoughts. But in general we aren't trained in that skill or in how to change our way of thinking. Instead, it's more likely we'll rationalize our thinking with the words: "That's just the way I am." We'd rather remain attached to our thought process and behavior as it is. Not being able to imagine thinking, feeling or acting differently than the way we currently are, in the face of a need for change, might be as good an example of *being stuck*.

Greg Snyder, a Zen Buddhist priest who runs youth meditation programs at the Brooklyn Zen Center, responds this way: "The only thing that keeps an emotion alive is your own thoughts. It's you, who keeps churning it over and over again. Your thoughts do not care about you. They only want to perpetuate themselves."

In his book, *What To Say When You Talk To Yourself,*[54] Shad Helmstetter, Ph.D. tells us that to make a permanent change you must have a different quality of self talk based on a *"new word-for-word set of instructions, new programming to the subconscious mind, the control center of the brain."* A friend of mine, Dr. Rick Hanson, Ph.D, a neuropsychologist who's written and taught about the essential inner skills of personal well-being, teaches how to beat our brain's *"negativity bias,"* which is like Velcro for nega-

tive experiences but Teflon for positive ones. What's more, correctly identifying the exact thought we want to change might be like catching a greased otter in a thick fog.

> It's more likely we'll rationalize our thinking with the words: "That's just the way I am."

> In my own consciousness, winning was kind of an abstract dream. Yet I also was determined to make the dream real.

INTERNAL DIALOG — MY OWN CASE STUDY

My own path to growth incorporated numerous of modalities: meditation, yoga, prayer, talk therapy, coaching, daily journaling ("Morning Pages,")* workshops, support groups, countless conversations and an amazing type of diagnostic healing called Proprioceptive-Deep Tendon Reflex[55] — to name a few. It took me a long time to see how negatively and unconsciously I was talking to myself and how significantly it impacted my behavior.

I ultimately realized something about my internal dialog: I had actually been listening to two different voices. The first was speaking in words, in a rational conversational voice I could listen in on. The second was expressing itself in more of a non-verbal way that could overpower the first voice. This second voice directed me with sensations, feelings and emotion to which I tended to respond almost like a puppet. But then, at certain points the second voice would let go of control and allow the voice of words and reason to guide me. The second voice was always negative; it conveyed a feeling of *can't* and a lack of acceptance. At one point the voice had such a menacing presence I referred to it as "IT".

"IT" was a presence or a feeling that made no rational sense to me. Its thought was: "I'm not okay. I can't win. All I can do is survive." "IT" was a *feeling* of striving, an embedded sense of defeat, victimhood and being lost. In my own consciousness, success was kind of an abstract dream. Yet I was determined to make that dream real.

* This stack of papers is a year and three months worth of my "Morning Pages" a daily three-page journaling process, part of "The Artist's Way" program designed by Julia Cameron.

RECOVERY — SHIFTING INTERNAL DIALOG

Over time and with outside help, I began to separate my sense of self from my negative thought patterns. Once I came to understand the trauma and emotional highjacking, I realized I could step back from and let go of them.

It might seem hard to believe that I operated in a state of emotional survival for most of my life without realizing it. But let's look at the major conditions in play: 1) I was functional at an acceptable level; 2) Unconsciously I would do almost anything not to feel pain or look bad; 3) I'd been operating on survival autopilot since infancy. While surviving might sometimes look like thriving, these are two *totally* different states. Though my own condition wasn't even comparable to the kind of dysfunction requiring drugs or other interventions, I carried a boatload of shame and avoidance around inside me for decades.

One of the biggest single steps was recognizing and owning the power of saying: "I am uncomfortable with this." How simple it sounds to say that now — but it didn't used to be that way for me.

To be sure, not everyone is looking for this kind of recovery. If you are, however, the sooner you can get on with it, the happier and more effective you'll be. The next step may be realizing: Hey, maybe I *am* ____ing myself with my own thoughts!

This is how virtually all gamechangers begin in life: with shifts in perception. Take a look and see what's true for *you* without applying any negative labels of non-acceptance. With *as much self-acceptance* and non-judgment as you can, focus precisely on what you want to change in your thinking — rather than on who you are. This may not be easy to do, but it's essential. That's why people journal or talk to the right support person.

> Hey, maybe I am ____ing myself with my own thoughts!

105

LOOKING EGO IN THE EYE

Ego expresses itself in countless ways. Three quick examples: 1) a person announcing: "I'm the greatest," 2) a humorous public poke, or 3) giving someone the silent treatment. We may hardly even think about such actions as expressions of ego, but they are. Is ego inherently good or bad? I believe it's inherently neutral, a dominating mental mechanism with two possible functions: to enable an individual to survive and/or thrive. As protector or driver, its often-silent battle cries are: "I avoid danger!" and "I do what I want!" It expresses emotions like humility, confidence, pride and arrogance. Wired very differently in each of us, ego usually functions as the pilot who determines how we see the world through a sense of identity. But just as often ego identity can be false, incomplete or limited. Yet ego is still largely something of a mystery. Ask any 10 people what they think ego is, how it works, or how important it is and you'll get 10 different answers. It's amazing actually, considering its invisible role and ongoing impact in our lives.

Online, Google gives us these synonyms for ego: self-esteem, self-importance, self-worth, self-respect, self-image, self-confidence. Macmillan online dictionary offers this definition: "the opinion that you have of yourself and your own importance, in psychology ... the conscious part of the mind that is responsible for thinking and understanding." Wikipedia provides the definition: "'Ego' is a Latin and Greek word meaning 'I,' in English the 'self,' 'identity' or other related concepts."

Sometimes ego shows up in personality assessments, in labels like alpha male or female, or in behavior profiles, like DISC, where the D stands for driver or dominator. Ego also shows up when we identify personal agendas, which are often discussed in bars after a meeting in which a big ego took over.

> Is ego inherently good or bad? I think it's inherently neutral. It exists with two main psychological aims: to survive and/or thrive.

"THE ENEMY AS EGO" VIDEO AND TRANSCRIPT

I invite you to watch an unusual video[56] (http://www.wimp.com/theego/) aided by the transcript below, in which eight different experts on psychology talk about the role of the ego. I've watched it at least a dozen times.

"The ego is the worst confidence trickster we could ever figure, we could ever imagine, because you don't see it ... And the single biggest con is: "I am you." ... The problem is that the ego hides in the last place that you'd ever look– within itself ... It disguises its thoughts as your thoughts, its feelings as your feelings. You think it's you ... People's need to protect their own egos knows no bounds. They will lie, cheat, steal, kill – do whatever it takes to maintain what we call 'ego boundaries' ... People have no clue that they're in prison. They don't know there's an ego. They don't know the distinction ... At first it's difficult for the mind to accept that there's something beyond itself, that there's something of greater value and greater capacity for discerning truth than itself ... In religion the ego manifests as the devil, and of course no one realizes how smart the ego is because it created the devil so we could blame someone else ... In creating this imaginary external enemy we made a real enemy for ourselves, and that becomes a real danger to the ego but that's also the ego's creation ... There is no such thing as an external enemy no matter what that voice in your head is telling you. All perception of an enemy is a projection of the ego as the enemy ... In that sense is to say that a hundred percent of our external enemies are of our own creation. Your greatest enemy is your own inner perception, is your own ignorance, is your own ego."

Dr. Yoav Datillo Ph.D., Dr, Steven Hayes, Ph.D., Dr. Peter Fonagy, Ph.D. FBA, Leonard Jacobson, Andrew Samuels, Ph.D. Dr.David Hawkins, MD, Ph.D, Dr.Deepak Chopra, Dr. Obadiah Harris, Ph.D.

> "It (ego) disguises its thoughts as your thoughts, *its* feelings as *your* feelings. You think it's you. . ."

CONSCIOUS WILL, MIND, BRAIN AND "HAVE-TO"

Meaningful change begins with . . .

1) Acknowledging the behavior or situation to be changed
2) Taking responsibility for that behavior or situation
3) Looking at your behavior or situation differently

From the moment we decide to get out of bed each day, we're exercising some degree of conscious will. Mainstream culture tells that conscious will resides inside each of us like a reservoir of emotional juice, ready to be accessed at the flick of a switch. If only we knew exactly where to find that switch when we need it most! Nothing we can physically see (yet) using brain scanning technology is known specifically to regulate this power. I think will is like emotional muscle strength wired a little differently into each mind. Whether using it is an act of choice, faith or habit, tapping into it is useful. One purpose of this book is to support you in connecting with and developing *your* conscious will for achieving desired behavior change — even if the exact "how-to-do-it" is still a mystery. How many times will you exercise yours today?

Modern neuroscience has already helped us map and understand the function of many brain structures (like the neocortex, limbic system, reptile brain, hippocampus, amygdala, etc.) and processes like "stimulus-response," "fight, flight or freeze," etc. New information arrives each day about the neurochemicals 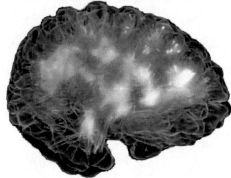 and neurotransmitters that invisibly influence the function of our brain and thus behavior. While undoubtedly there are particular physical brain structures related to the functioning of conscious

> Mainstream culture even tells us that conscious will resides inside each of us like a reservoir of emotional juice, ready to be accessed at the flick of a switch.

will, to my knowledge neuroscience hasn't yet revealed the details of their operation. Whether we understand it intellectually or not, each of us has abundant opportunity to experiment with our will to master its workings within us. Personally, I'd start with meditation as a foundation for this awareness.

What is will exactly? How can you dial it up or down? How long do you have from the time you have an impulse to do something about it before it's lost? What does it take to overcome, change or replace a "bad" habit with a good one? Goldsmith's *Triggers*, Duhigg's *Habits*, Covey's *7 Habits*, and McGonigal's *Superbetter* sit among the shelves of books that dig deeply into this subject.

For centuries, our greatest teachers, theologians, philosophers, thought leaders and authors have formulated positions about conscious will. From Socrates' instruction: "Know thyself," to Shakespeare's line from Hamlet: "To thine own self be true," millions of people have pursued authentic expression of their will. Many others meanwhile seem to struggle with lifelong patterns in which they can't seem to find enough of their own will.

When you act on an impulse related to your desired change, is it because you consciously choose to do that thing, or because in some way you are conditioned or feel obligated, or are in state of reaction? Take a moment to reflect on this question — long enough to really look without judgment at your answer to this question. For greater command over your life you need to find an answer or two that enables you to act authentically. What is *your* current awareness telling you?

> From Socrates' instruction: "Know thyself" to Shakespeare's "To thine own self be true," millions of people have pursued the authentic expression of their will and desire.

STUCK = NOT MOVING. Unlike cars caught in traffic jams or mud holes, we humans often get stuck in our own mental or emotional loops.

ENERGY AND MOVEMENT (PLAY - FLOW - FUN)

Desired behavior change requires flexing, stretching, imagining and allowing — in short: movement. It's what most of us are built for and thrive on! It's why people love movement in every form imaginable: from dancing to skiing, running to yoga, design to photography and let's not forget about travel. So right now, if you're reading this and sitting down, put on some music, if you're not already listening, and get your torso moving to a beat that makes you move. Here's what I'm listening to while writing this: http://app.rhapsody.com/artist/colbie-caillat/album/all-of-you/track/brighter-than-the-sun. I challenge you not to move if you listen to it.

NOT MOVING = STUCK. Unlike cars caught in traffic jams or mud holes, we humans often get stuck in our own mental or emotional loops. Once we realize we're in a loop, we need to have a mechanism to assist us out of it, or ask for help. We need to *see* that loop and how it works — how we get triggered — and *exactly* how it trips us up. Not seeing these steps makes us easily subject to the chronic victimizing effect of that loop. Again, visualizing can be a key to action. Could you — if I asked — sketch an image of some kind that would visually represent your stuck loop?

STUCK . . . BLOCKED . . . JAMMED?

There's no fun in being stuck — in traffic, your bed, your head, in a job or relationship you don't like — because there's no movement, no progress. Movement is an antidote to feeling stuck. Release and progress are results. I observe that movement can sometimes be achieved as simply as changing even one thought, or moving my body when I feel tense or gripped. Another antidote to feeling stuck for me is expressing something like: "Hold on a second, I need to take a moment." Then I take a couple of conscious breaths. If possible, I think of something funny enough to make me laugh. Any of these can do the trick.

What are some stuckness-freeing thoughts or moves for you? Whatever they are, *use* them! If and when you feel stuck, get on your feet, drum on your desk, breathe deeply (more on this later), tell the truth, laugh, help someone else, sing a song, change your state. Shift something — anything to get out of that loop.

Each of us is an ever-changing energy scenario. When we feel most alive and at our best is when our energy is flowing, moving, unblocked — like water. When our energy is reduced or jammed up past a certain point, then we're NOT flowing and it doesn't feel good — because *we're made to move!*

When you FEEL stuck, get on your feet, drum on your desk, breathe deeply, tell the truth, laugh, help someone else, sing a song, change your state.

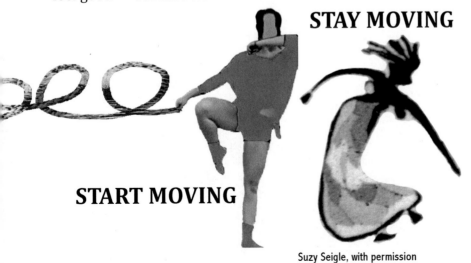

STAY MOVING

START MOVING

Suzy Seigle, with permission

111

MINDFULNESS, STILLNESS, PRESENCE, ATTENTION

Not everyone has an easy time going inward, being still, reflective or quiet. It's a practice that isn't universally easy. Some of us work on it for a lifetime — through yoga, meditation, writing, music, even crafts. Sometimes we must go into nature, visit a church or temple, garden, the water's edge, or take a walk. Wherever you can find stillness is good, even if it's in a crowd. Reducing internal noise to discern what's most real to your heart and spirit may be part of achieving desired change for you.

The practice of **mindfulness** is slowly emerging in our culture. You may have heard of it being employed in the workplace to alleviate or reduce stress and improve focus. Mindfulness is a practice of calmly and intently developing a moment-by-moment awareness with full appreciation of what you're doing. Mindfulness practice, inherited from the Buddhist tradition, can enhance your sense of well being as it increases your productivity.[57]

Presence is the quality of being whole, undistracted, focused and attentive to what's in front of you. Your mind isn't elsewhere. You care about whatever or whomever is in front of you. Giving to yourself in this way, whether it's an audience or your kids, demonstrates a very real kind of power, says Harvard professor

and social psychologst, Amy Cuddy.[58] People feel it, too, both consciously and unconsciously. It means "bringing your boldest self to your biggest challenges."

> Presence is the quality of being whole, powerful, undistracted, focused and attentive to what's in front of you.

BREATHING — RECEIVE . . . ENJOY . . . LAUGH!*

Your breath is your lifeline. Increasing the practice of conscious breathing is perhaps the single fastest, easiest, least-expensive way to improve your state. It will move you from fight, flight or freeze to greater choice in an instant. Yoga and meditation, which are based on breathing, have made a huge difference in tens of millions of lives. Even Google teaches mindfulness to its employees.[59] My own breath practices have led me to develop and facilitate an engaging corporate wellness and productivity program called **"Connection 101."** [60]

Here's what we know about mindful, focused breathing. It:

1. Costs nothing
2. Works immediately
3. Appeals to everyone
4. Is easy and fun to learn
5. Enhances communication
6. Rejuvenates mind and body
7. **Releases and reduces stress**
8. Improves morale and teamwork
9. Enables better focus and concentration
10. Develops greater wellness, vitality & energy
11. Strengthens peer-to-peer and top-down support
12. Lessens reactive behavior that often disrupts workflow

While such benefits might strongly suggest making conscious breathing a best practice in the workplace, it hasn't yet become a priority for many companies. If you're thinking of asking *your* company to consider this multi-purpose culture-builder, remember to relax and smile.

Conscious mindful breathing lessens reactive behavior that often disrupts work flow.

* This series might also include singing and possibly dancing as well.

113

> The further we get from real — in our heads and behind enemy lines — the more difficult it is to make real change.

PHYSICALITY — ALSO KNOWN AS PRESENCE

Extending mindfulness a step further, let's talk about an awareness of what I call "physicality." Think of the word visceral. This awareness allows you to instantly grasp the degree to which any given experience is *real* to you — versus abstract, conceptual, mental, intellectual, etc. Our thoughts and minds can play some real tricks on us. Physicality means feeling the truth about something, not just thinking it; In the context of change, it's useful to realize that the further we get from real — *in our heads and behind enemy lines* — the more difficult it is to make real change. Awareness of physicality can make a game-changing difference.

When an insight or new perception is actionable and likely to stick, it hits us physically or emotionally. If an insight is only "in our head," it passes through our mind and doesn't take hold. It doesn't become action. I refer to this as "having a good idea." It has no physicality. It's not usually a shared experience, either. I might hear it coming from your mouth, but I don't "get it." Example: You might tell me you're going to start being more punctual. But if what I experience from you is just a "good idea" and not real, then I'm not going to buy it, and you won't either.

Stegnor's pile of gloves (pages 41-43) enabled his executives to get the physicality reality. In minutes, huge invisible complexity became so real and clear that decisive and effective action was taken almost immediately. This is the power of presence. Think of it as Presence 2.0.

Physicality: The reality of the situation vs. what's in our mind, or our (limited) perception?

114

ACCOUNTABILITY AND CONSEQUENCES

When Clarity, Connection, Conditions and Motivation are all in place, you'll see Action. Once you're set on achieving that change — or any real accomplishment — you have to work for it and practice it diligently. It's a one-step-after-another proposition . . . to work out the kinks, eliminate resistance and make the change sustainable. Success factors include time, support, feedback and an unwavering sense of ownership and responsibility. When one of these factors is missing, you won't get sustained effective action or change. How you perceive external "good" or "bad" consequences can also strongly influence the degree to which you feel motivated or not. In traditional terms, think "reward and punishment" here. In the world of business it's called accountability.

Changes in me that resulted in my writing this book have taken place one day, hour, minute and inner conversation at a time, as they have for practicing yoga, reducing my procrastination, being prompt, or lessening the sugar I eat. As Walter Schneider said on page 95: the key is "discipline." Developing even a discipline you need might require a support system just for that.

Ensuring your effective action can come down to "owning" or creating the conditions that will enable a sustainable practice of your desired change. Will you be fully honest with yourself about what those conditions are and how you're meeting them?

What are YOUR conditions and consequences?

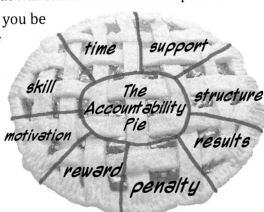

time | support
skill
The Accountability Pie
structure
motivation
results
reward
penalty

How you perceive external "good" or "bad" consequences can strongly influence the degree to which you feel motivated or not.

> Know and understand exactly where your best ideas, intentions or plans can go astray, where you can get sidetracked, lose focus or get highjacked.

7-TIP ROUNDUP FOR ACCELERATING CHANGE

Let's pause for an overview of some step-by-step basics.

First, recognize and resolve that if you're going to effect a change it begins with you — not with anyone or anything else.

Second, look at yourself and your situation differently.

Third, commit to actually *doing* something different — in small steps, one moment, interaction, challenge or opportunity at a time. Example: being on time. Plan to be early enough to account for contingencies like extra-heavy traffic, remembering something you've forgotten, a printer breaking down at the 11th hour, needing to grab a bite because you haven't eaten, a last-minute call, or just plain "running late," etc. Commit to leaving for appointments at least 50 percent earlier than you think you need to.

Fourth, identify sources of support and ask for the help you need.

Fifth, when you take a step, acknowledge it and share it with others to whom it will make a difference. Acknowledge and build upon any "bright spots" or wins — whatever they are.

Sixth, make choices that ensure your integrity and help guarantee delivery of your highest intended outcome. The executive producer of HBO's successful program, "The Newsroom," once told me: "All anyone is going to remember is: Was it a good episode? They won't recall or think about how much it cost."

Seventh, know and understand where your best ideas, intentions or plans can go astray, where you can lose focus or get highjacked. Anticipate a negative trigger could be pulled. No one wants to plan for something to go wrong, but in the realm of human change, that's exactly what you need to do. We're human. We slip; the chances are great that it's going to happen.

JUMPING IN AND STAYING INSPIRED

How much commitment can you muster? What kind of support can you ask for? How passionately, tenaciously and dependably can you hold that desired end result in your mind?

You know it won't always be easy or comfortable. So you must stoke your engine with one kind of inspiration after another, keeping yourself continually fueled with "the real thing," by recognizing the physicality (page 114) of what you find inspirational. External motivation can work beautifully for short bursts, but it flames out as you get distracted with a setback or emotional hijacking. Only when you develop the habit of keeping the internal logs of inspiration burning in your boiler do you have the

immediate power to overcome obstacles. How can there be too many ways to stay inspired? The trick is to use one at a time: books, Internet, social media, your favorite music, a breathing break, movement, doing something wonderful for another human being. Even inspiration takes pacing! With so many websites sending out an inspiring daily message, maybe one of them is for you!

> Only when you develop the habit of keeping the internal logs of inspiration burning in your boiler, do you have the immediate power to overcome obstacles.

> Aided by your imagination, almost everything you do stems from your sense of possibility and power — or a lack of it.

WHO WE ARE — LIMITED OR UNLIMITED?

Consider the metaphor of a person as a two-sided coin. On one side we feel *unlimited* in what we can do — boundless. On the other side we experience a limited or restricted sense of power. On side A, you can imagine something is difficult, yet possible to achieve; on side B, you stop yourself from even trying. Which side are you on? An amazing demonstration of side A can be seen in the personal victory for quadriplegic Kyle Maynard, who bear-crawled to the top of Africa's Mt. Kilimanjaro 19,341-foot summit in 2012. (http://thechart.blogs.cnn.com/2011/11/08/human-factor-a-goal-is-a-direction-not-an-end/) Is there a personal aha! for *you* here?

Aided by your imagination, almost everything you do stems from your sense of possibility — or the lack of it. What determines this sense comes from your own personal sense of *"who you are"* — all you're capable of being in this lifetime. (Remember the Well?) If reading this book triggers a new understanding of your unique potential, then you're already *getting out of your own box!* The "Nine Dots Model" is an exercise (and another metaphor) in seeing the possibility within you differently.

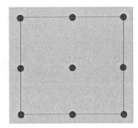

The thin green line outlining the square defines the box. The challenge is to connect the nine dots using only four connected lines without taking your pencil off the paper. It's done by moving completely outside the box. Try it with a pencil. You'll find the answer on page 146 in the Appendix.

WHO WE ARE — USED AND UNUSED POTENTIAL

At 50 years old, the Esalen Institute in Big Sur, CA. (www.esalen.org) is perhaps the longest-running, leading-edge human potential development center in the world. After its first 30 years of work, its two founders, Michael Murphy and George Leonard, wrote the book, *The Life We Are Given*, to review what they'd learned over three decades. They concluded that the single biggest missing element of most long-term change programs was ongoing peer support. Then they conducted a significant research program to validate it. "We live only part of the life we are given," said Murphy and Leonard. "Whatever your age, your upbringing, or your education, what you are made of is mostly unused potential."[61] Their message is: "Who we are is a one-of-a-kind unfolding miracle few of us ever fully realize." Seeing this miracle every day helps you lead a richer and fuller life each day, whether you're using your full potential or not.

How clearly do you see it and enroll others in helping you fulfill *your* potential? One key to realizing that inner potential is sharing with each other the process of facing our challenges: sharing our dreams, goals, strengths, fears, etc. with people we respect, who can and want to help us. Will *you* do that? Let's see!

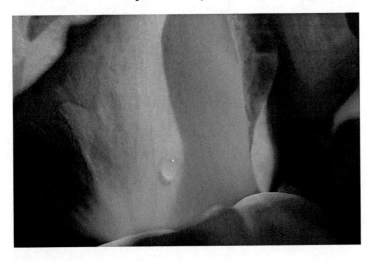

> "Who we are is a one-of-a-kind unfolding miracle few of us ever fully realize."

> You can tackle almost any personal issue or achieve almost any desired behavior change if you can stand back and look at yourself differently.

SHARING IT

We've reached the end of the GameChangers section. Can you see these five keys in your mind's eye? Can you pull any of them out of your memory and into use as easily as your cell phone? One thing that will help with your future practice of these keys is sharing your learning with people. Let me suggest an action plan.

EXPLORATORY EXERCISE #14 – QUICK SCRIPT

Take a few minutes to write out a 15-second script in your own words that allows you to share the value of the GameChangers with someone else. It might sound something like this:

Did you know you can tackle almost any personal issue or achieve any desired behavior change if you stand back and look at yourself differently? If you can see things from another point of view, your mind and emotions will enable you to shift.

_____

_____

_____

_____

Short of having an app downloaded into your brain, here's a visual you can use any time, as fast as 1-2-3-4-5 to help you recall and determine what's missing in your own or anyone else's change process.

conditions · motivation · connection · action · clarity

120

9
CONCLUSION AND NEXT STEPS

This final chapter is a collection of reminders and reference points for taking action and making your desired change real. Each one is a slightly different supplement to what I've suggested previously.

If just one of these many processes works for you it will deliver big results. Be sure to take a look at each activity and see if in some way you can "get" the essence of that process before moving on. It's not the words the are important; it's their meaning that you want to make yours. Make the meaning yours and you'll have the right process at your command when you need it.

It's not the words that are important. It's their meaning that you want to make yours. Make *the why* — their meaning — yours, and you'll find the right process when you need it.

REVIEWING THE TOP PREDICTORS

Which of the many perspectives we've explored do you think are essential to remember and practice? Here are my own top eight.

Predictor #1 – **Assess You're Readiness and Motivation**
Why do you think you're truly motivated? Are all the conditions, including support, in place and in your favor?

Predictor #2 – **Feel Your Feelings**
Achieving desired change requires *feeling* your emotions more than thinking them. A close friend, associate and executive coach tells me that getting people to feel and express what's going on with them physically and emotionally is one of the most challenging things for most people to do. Remember what Obi-wan says in Star Wars: "*Feel* the force, Luke!" He doesn't say: "Think about it."

Predictor #3 – **Tell the Truth With Respect and No Judgment**
This is the fastest way to be clear, authentic and move it forward.

Predictor #4 – **Change Your Perception**
This is where change begins, where we get the traction to move.

Predictor #5 – **Let It Go**
Accept it, forgive it, say goodbye to, complete or eliminate it, etc.

Predictor #6 – **Lean Into Your Discomfort**
Allow and move through the feeling of discomfort" ("Ouch! This doesn't feel good.") when it comes — *and it will come.*

Predictor #7 – **Get Support**
The right connections and relationships make all the difference.

Predictor #8 – **Breathe, Move and Expand Your Appreciation**
We're meant for movement, the antidote to feeling stuck. The more gratitude we can feel for every breath and movement, the better.

> Which of the perspectives would make your top predictor list? Write them down and make them yours.

PLANNING — GOALS → STRATEGIES → LOGISTICS

Hopefully you now have at least one behavior change goal that will help turn your individual dream, or that of your team, into reality faster. Sometimes what's missing from the desired change process are planning tools that make implementation more predictable: a flow chart, schedule, checklist, declaration, etc. Tools like these must be *seen* — visible to the eye on paper, screen or whiteboard — and shared. Making things visible provides credibility, specificity, concreteness, etc., thus greater predictability in achieving that goal. (see also Footnote 9)

Planning moves you from the more general and abstract to the more concrete and specific. Plans can help keep you on track. By the time you're done planning the logistics — who does what, where, when, how, etc. — you're ready for action. At that point, if you haven't already done so, you have to ask yourself honestly: Why wouldn't this happen? What can or will get in the way? Your answer may confront you with two critical issues:

1) You, or your team may lack the motivation needed.
2) You've done no "What-if," "Plan B" contingency planning.

Because effective planning can be tedious and confrontive, it demands you stick with it when you might rather bolt. I've seen planning avoidance and "excusitis" undermine team effectiveness too many times. Such avoidance is insidious, like a slow leak. It's the reason for the old saying: "When you fail to plan, you plan to fail." We knowingly allow it to happen over time.

"We are all faced with a series of great opportunities brilliantly disguised as insoluble problems."

John W. Gardener, 1912-2002 US Secretary of Health, Education & Welfare

Planning tools must be *seen* — visible to the eye on paper, screen or whiteboard — and shared.

123

Often letting something go feels like the last thing you want to do, whether you call it acceptance, forgiveness, a breakthrough or taking the high road.

LETTING THINGS GO — A REVIEW

When it comes to transformation, I've found we almost always have to do one if not two kinds of work: 1) Inside work — on ourselves, 2) Outside work — on relationships or things. Inside work is usually more difficult. Letting go is mainly inside work.

In its simplest form, the emotional work I'm talking about means admitting something, or releasing or letting go of your position, story, point of view, etc. Letting something go can feel like the last thing you want to do, whether you call it acceptance, forgiveness, a breakthrough or taking the high road. When making desired behavior changes, you know you have free choice, but (let's face it) you may not exercise that choice as much or as easily as you'd generally like to. Not letting go might be the reason.

Here's a little Letting-Go Test. Have you ever gone through this three-part cycle, or something similar, quickly? You probably have.

Oh shit!
Oh God!
Oh well!

We can all find countless examples of people getting unstuck or off it in some way, from business to our personal lives, but it's not often openly discussed — and least of all in government, politics or mainstream media. The documentary, *Mandela: The Long Walk to Freedom* (2013), recounts Nelson Mandela's incredible return from 27 years in prison. In a passionate emergency television message to his countrymen at the height of internal conflict, he asked South African blacks to forgive Afrikaners' past transgressions in order to move into the future. Mandela's act of motivating an entire majority population to forgive their persecutors may be unprecedented in history.

To take a new breath, we must release the previous one. To form a new habit, we must say goodbye to or write over the old one. Example: If I really want to reduce the number of cookies I consume each day, I have to supply something to my ego that satisfies it as much as cookies when my stress or anxiety are triggered. If I don't, my desired *Fewer Cookies Habit* won't take hold. I have to work with the unconscious mechanisms in me. What does my ego really want most? Answer: Control of, or relief from the anxiety triggered by the stress — not the sweet! The sugar hit is only a moment's relief. In reality, eating that sweet reduces my real control because I'll likely feel sluggish in 20 minutes.

Conquering the anxiety is a steeper hill. First, I have to see that the behavior in question — eating cookies — isn't working. Letting go of that, including the positions "I'm right," or "I deserve this," are part of the process though tougher to do. That's why we need plenty of laughter, self-acceptance, support or clear consequences. I invite you to read the short essay I wrote on "Letting Things Go as a Best Practice", on pages 158-59.

Awareness by itself doesn't guarantee the change, release or freedom we seek. It's the *shift* in our perception that usually begins our transformation. That's why we need a conscious if not emotional (sometimes even physical) letting go process — which takes practice. It's this letting go that feels risky, humbling or challenging. The battle is within our own psyche. Our ego digs in, screaming: "I'm right! I shouldn't have to let go of this or take ownership of that. I'm me and I deserve to get my way!" But ultimately, letting go only tends to hurt for a few moments when we finally do it. Then we can move on, feeling free and empowered.

Most of us have the capacity to sigh, laugh or throw a few ornery words at what disturbs us. Then, maybe, we can let go and get

> To move forward, we first have to fully accept the fact that the behavior in question isn't actually working.

on with things quickly. However, we don't always act on that capacity in a timely way. Sometimes it feels emotionally easier to hang on to what's bothering us and remain stuck in it. We might need to feel right for a while — even a long while. When that happens, who cares about perceptual or behavioral flexibility? We just want to sulk, blame someone or scream. Anger is often another form of that reflexive fight response to a threat. It's hard to mask it. In some way, shape or form we want to strike back, in effect saying: "Go #&%! yourself!"— the opposite of letting go.

Regardless of how much you might *need* to let go of something, you can also inwardly ask for help in letting go of whatever you no longer *want*. The acronym **AIM** has helped me in this process. AIM is a request you can make of *yourself* or your higher power, spirit, etc. It stands for: **Awaken** (or Activate, Allow, Aliven or Actualize) **In Me**[62]. . . and then you list what you want. For example, I have asked: Awaken in me the ability to let go of my procrastination. This is a simple and humble request that you can say aloud or inwardly often with as much conviction as you want. Let it speak to your mind, your heart, something outside yourself or all three. In essence, it's a form of letting go, acceptance and connection.

> That's why we need a conscious if not emotional (even physical) letting go process — and it takes practice.

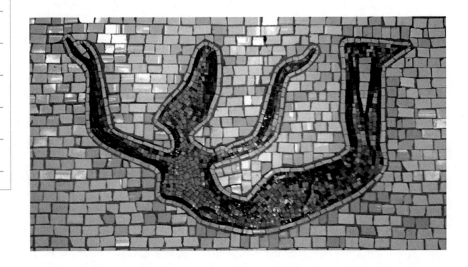

126

END GAMES

Around a corner, when you're least expecting it, someone may throw a question your way, which you may want to be ready for sooner than later. The question is: What's your end game? What long-term result do you most want to create or achieve as the biggest possible outcome of your purpose or passion? Asked in a slightly different way, the question is: What do you want to be known most for achieving or accomplishing? What result would bring the greatest joy to your heart, make a difference in the world, fulfill you, and express who you are and what's possible?

Ideally your answer will bowl people over because it taps into that biggest possible you. They'll get it in a way that instantly tells them you're inspired, serious and capable. In this way, you can enroll others in some way in helping you to achieve that end game. In case you didn't know it, *unexpected, creative or out-of-the-box answers* are the ones that inspire people most.

Coaching and strategic planning with outside professionals prepares us to answer those questions. Wrestling with them inside ourselves connects us with our long-term trajectory even more. One of my end games, in addition to public speaking, coaching, training and facilitating, is an innovative business model I call Connections Urban Retreat & Studio. You can read about it on pages 144-145.

> What long-term result do you most want to create or achieve as the biggest possible outcome of your purpose or passion?

127

> No one kind of moment is better than another; they're all great.

Seth Green, Rally's spot Photo: YouTube

CHA-CHING MOMENTS

On page 27 we talked about making **measurement** your ally, and in EXPLORATORY EXERCISE #3 on page 28 I suggested you list at least three things you could measure involving your desired change item. Example: If your desired change was to get out of bed 30 minutes earlier each day, you might have said:

1. # of times that week I set my alarm for 30 minutes earlier.
2. # of times that week I went to bed earlier.
3. # of times I managed to actually get out of bed earlier.
4. Amount of time I spent preparing for a great night's sleep.
5. Rewards I might give myself for doing it (measurable).
6. What that 30 minutes of time enabled me to do or feel.

You could also turn this activity or any feelings it resulted in, into a subjective (1-10) rating system for yourself — in chart form even.

Here's a simple, out-of-the-box challenge I invite you to have fun with over a week or two — if not a month or the rest of your life. I call it the **Cha-Ching Challenge,** based on an irreverent popular 1991 commercial for Rally's, a local drive-through, which starred a young Seth Green, that become a well-known idiomatic expression over the last 25 years. Here's the challenge:

Imagine in your mind all the emotions, sensations and experiences you enjoy feeling and want to feel as much as possible: joy, happiness, connection, generosity, relatedness, energy, aliveness, spontaneity, authenticity, etc. You may even want to make a list of them. We're going to call this set of feelings "Cha-Ching Moments" because they make you feel richer in life, blessed, fortunate, etc. No one kind of moment is better than another; they're all great. So great in fact that one Cha-Ching Moment can make your day. Some people, on some days, may not feel like they have any, yet ultimately you can learn to generate as many of them as you want. How long is a moment, you might ask? Ten seconds, two minutes? It's up to you. Life is made of moments. If you're awake 16 hours a day and you consider a moment to be one minute long, you have nearly *1,000* moments a day!

Here's the challenge. It has six steps. What's essential is the first:

1) Create or allow yourself as many Cha-Ching Moments as you can in a day, so at the end of the day you feel filled-up and energized by them. Some of these you'll share, if not co-create with others — the more the better of course. See if you can increase the number of them each day.

2) Keep track of these moments as best you can. I suggest even making quick notes about some of them. At the end of the day, you want to be able to recall at least a few, and roughly how many. You can journal them if it strikes you to do so.

3) Share your moments with someone. It doesn't have to be all or most of your moments, but at least one, or a few.

4) Enroll others to join you in this process. At the end of a day, ask at least one of your Cha-Ching buddies how many Cha-Ching Moments they enjoyed, then share a Cha-Ching story or two.

5) Help create a Cha-Ching Moment *for* at least one other person each day. How you manage to do that is up to you.

6) Observe what comes up for you over the first week. Will it become a wonderful tradition or a chore-bore? Let's see!

I invite you to use the two pages that follow as a guide and a place to journal your experience.

> How long is a moment you might ask? Ten seconds, two minutes? That's up to you.
> Life is made of moments.

CHA-CHING CHALLENGE JOURNAL

(NOTE: These categories are suggested here to spark your imagination and sense of possibility.

JOY & SPONTANEITY	HEALTH & VITALITY	KINDNESS & SUPPORT

You can fill them in with others that have greater meaning — or you don't need any categories at all.

ACKNOWLEDGEMENT	DESIRED CHANGE	PRODUCTIVITY

THE NEW NORMAL — STRESSED, A LITTLE CRAZY AND BEING HONEST ABOUT IT

Our skill in effectively navigating the currents of change hinges on how well we can swim in choppy waters, i.e., difficult times. But let's be honest, in Western culture, especially the U.S., we don't *always* tell-it-like-it-is — for several reasons. First: who wants to hear it all? We're likely not surrounded by people who have either the interest or bandwidth to take in all the details of our lives. So we keep putting on our game face and making things sound fine and acceptable. Second: we know the world is or could be judging us at any moment — 24/7. Maintaining appearances and creating the right impression have become the norm. Third: almost everyone colludes in a process of generalizing in some way, from the press to the president. It's the game the world is conditioned to play.

Almost everyone I know today, at one point or another, feels at least "a little crazy." Crazy is a term that means a lot of things — some of them even good. It's okay when we observe someone, even jokingly, openly own this state with a knowing smile and a desire for a bit of empathy. It could be, however, that their actual overall situation is more delicate. Our common idea of "crazy" spans from moody, scattered, fragmented, or overwhelmed all the way to persistent forms of chronic stress and anxiety, which can render people dysfunctional or dangerously ready to snap.

Generally speaking, we all know what day-to-day, in-the-moment crazy looks like — having a bit too many things on our plate. What we often can't see, however, is how fragile an underlying situation might be, and the stress that's building or has already built to a breaking point. That's what we need to be extra

> Almost everyone I know today, at one point or another, feels at least "a little crazy."

mindful of — because that seemingly harmless state of "crazy" might be a breakdown waiting to happen. Let's also consider how much energy is needed just to "keep it together" and survive. We may not feel we even have the bandwidth to step back and take stock of the state we're in, let alone make the kind of desired behavior changes we've been discussing here.

Crazy seems to be a condition of the plugged-in, 24/7, ever-faster computer age. We're pushed by the seeming acceleration of time, but it's really the pace of change that's speeding up. Our attention is being sucked up far more by technical or system issues, too. The question is: Just how crazy are we? There's no way to calibrate it without getting into an ever-extending zone of ambiguity. But you may be aware of the statistic that one in five people will experience some form of mental illness in their lifetime. According to Brené Brown, we are the most in-debt, obese, addicted and medicated adult cohort in U.S. history. As a population we can probably use some additional self-help. What do you think?

In his book, *In Praise Of Slowness: Challenging the Cult of Speed*, Carl Honore echoes Brown's observation: "Living on the edge of exhaustion, we are constantly reminded by our bodies and minds that the pace of life is spinning out of control."[63]

What can we do to prevent this cultural and individual craziness from overtaking us? Taking action on any of the suggestions in this book will begin making a positive difference almost immediately. Which one(s) might you undertake? How about simply taking 30 more conscious breaths a day? That's one extra-mindful and intentional breath every 30 minutes. *Want to try it?* Make this extra breath a Cha-Ching Moment for yourself.

> What can we do to prevent this cultural and individual craziness from overtaking us?

HIGHER CALLING AND TRUE IDENTITY

One of the best approaches to desired change I know can be found in what some people call higher purpose or calling, working for the greater common good or benefit to all. What if this is what we humans have been designed to do in some way? Our personal identity might be enhanced with every act of kindness and community service we perform. Might each of us embrace this aim given there's no limit to the good we can do? I believe this is a part of our design in the seen and unseen human laboratory.

While this may sound altruistic, it's actually in our own interest to serve the greater good. It makes us better people; it deepens, enriches and adds meaning to our lives. Connection and caring are the aims of every spiritual discipline. Greater good can be at our place of work, in our neighborhood, a special population in our community, or any situation where we can help. The scale doesn't matter either; what matters is touching others positively.

How does working for a greater good relate to desired behavior change? One of the fastest ways to get out of your own head is to assist someone else. *"The greatest good you can do for another is not just to share your riches, but to reveal to him his own,"* said Benjamin Disraeli, a famous British prime minister in the 1800s."[64]

"The greatest good you can do for another is not just to share your riches, but to reveal to him his own."

A tree planting event put on by TreePeople in Pacific Palisades, 2001.

COACHING — TWO APPROACHES

First: Getting Support

Knowing the kind of support you need, then *asking for* and getting it, requires high self-awareness plus guts. There's risk involved. Can you ask for the support you want with curiosity and without expectation? Can you ask with some lightness, even a little humor? Can you impart to the person you're asking that you're not going to react negatively or defensively to their input? Doing this means you're open, vulnerable and grateful. It will reflect your authenticity and earn his respect. On the other hand, if you have a reaction that causes the person who's your sounding board to feel threatened in any way, you may end up losing that person's willingness to be fully honest with you.

Example: Bob, would you be willing to help me with something? I need a reminder here and there to stop, take a breath and ask myself: Hey, what's going on with me? Just a quick check once a day maybe would serve me well, especially if you see that I'm getting a little stressed-out by something. Are you willing to ask me this question some time in the course of each day?

Second: Asking Questions

As Marshall Goldsmith illustrates in *Triggers,* if you're going to get effective coaching, the person who's coaching would serve you more by asking subjective *feeling* kinds of questions than by telling you what to do. The best coaching questions take insight to ask as well as to answer. They're the kinds of questions that cause you feel empowered rather than guilty or inadequate. Questions like: *How did you feel about doing that?* will lead to greater self-awareness and give you more access to your authenticity and effectiveness.

> Can you ask for the support you want with curiosity and without expectation? Can you ask with some lightness, even a little humor?

WHOLENESS, ONENESS AND CONNECTEDNESS

Faster than you can say "boo!", one little word — *love* — can pull a trigger or push a negative button for people in the workplace. But it doesn't have to. Instead, we can understand love as wholeness, oneness and connectedness — states that are universally desired. This definition can shift us away from any sexual, romantic or otherwise inappropriate associations. Clearly it's the *unwanted* advance or innuendo in the workplace that demonstrates a disconnection or lack of respect and oneness in the first place. As defined above, love is almost an intrinsic part of desired behavior change given it touches on all GameChangers. It is a powerful, practical, universal principle when we make connectedness or a passion for what we do a noble aim at work.

Years ago I was facilitating a group of managers at a corporate retreat. We'd been clearing the air for a couple of hours, and as

they were returning from a break, I decided to conduct a little experiment. Before the session started up again, I casually asked

> We can understand love as wholeness, oneness and connectedness — states that are universally desired.

several of them sitting at the table: "Do you think the word *love* has any place in business? In seconds their energy went from relaxed and open to tense and guarded. "No!" two of them blurted out. "We can never use that word in business. Absolutely not!"

In a *Harvard Business Review* article, "Primal Leadership: The Hidden Driver of Great Performance,"[65] three notable authors, including Daniel Goleman, make a strong, research-based case for leaders to realize that: "...of all the elements affecting bottom-line performance, the importance of the leader's mood and its attendant behaviors are most surprising...a leader's emotional state drives performance." The cause-and-effect relationships explored in the article speak directly to wholeness, oneness and connectedness as key factors in organizational productivity.

Why does it seem we have to fight to achieve or maintain wholeness, oneness and connectedness in business? Why are these conditions so easily undone when they take so much time and effort to create? As you may have guessed, it's about trust — created through caring, honesty, dependability, vulnerability, etc.

Whole-hearted living is recognized universally on this planet as essential to health and well being. Cultivating heart in appropriate forms means more moments that we feel and act on our connectedness. Perhaps above all, it means taking a certain kind of action.

Austin businessman, Roy Spence, reading to kids at the Texas book fair.

> Whole-hearted living is recognized universally on this planet as essential to health and well being.

137

EMBRACING THE ADVENTURE OF DESIRED CHANGE

Day-by-day, action-by-action, situation-by-situation, as you lean into your discomfort, you'll develop what it takes to achieve desired behavior change skillfully. Along the way, you'll want to look for any little "bright spots" of accomplishment and movement forward you can find as evidence of progress. Whether you want to yell out Tarzan's "call of the Wild" or "Yehaah!" the meaning is still: "Here I come, world! Watch out!"

Since it's natural at times to forget who we are, our purpose in life or the gifts we've been given, we can re-condition ourselves for those countless forgetful moments. These are the moments when we might stop to remember what humanitarian, Helen Keller [66] observed, that: "Life is either a daring adventure or nothing at all." Or we can pause to invoke that wonderful Navy SEAL expression: "Embrace the suck!" Or remember that any of these practices can begin with taking a conscious breath and filling yourself with gratitude as well as a lungful of oxygen.

> Remember that any of these practices can begin with taking a conscious breath and filling yourself with gratitude as well as oxygen.

As we glide into our conclusion and one final exercise, you might be interested in taking a look at what you wrote in that box-checking exercise (#2) on page 15? Find it now, and see if what you wrote then compares to what you're thinking and feeling about your desired behavior change at this moment.

EXPLORATORY EXERCISE #15 - LETTING GO

A final exercise to build your self-change muscles:

Write here what you're going to let go of first to achieve your desired change goal! Then share it with someone you respect. Do it as soon as you can (like right now.) Reach out to someone. Review as necessary until it's achieved!

_____

_____

_____

A nugget before some parting thoughts.

Our deepest fear is not that we are inadequate.
Our deepest fear is that we are powerful beyond measure.
It is our light, not our darkness that most frightens us.
We ask ourselves, Who am I to be brilliant, gorgeous,
    talented and fabulous?
Actually, who are you not to be? You are a child of God.
Your playing small does not serve the world.
There is nothing enlightened about shrinking so that other
    people will not feel insecure around you.

> Marianne Williamson,
> A Return to Love: Reflections on the Principles of "A Course in Miracles,"
> Chapter 7, Section 3, p. 190. (1992)

"Your playing small does not serve the world."

HERE'S TO YOUR AMAZING SUCCESS!

PARTING THOUGHTS

If you've reached a point of readiness, the conditions have been right and this book has done its work, you may have already shifted something — or you're getting ready to. Whether your change is simple, difficult, in the distant future or around the corner, let's give it a boost with one last personal story and an invitation.

First, the story. Prior to finishing the book, I observed myself starting to question the quality of my writing. Had I written clearly, thoughtfully and authentically enough? What further improvements could I make? Sure, thoughts like these might be expected for any author, but that's when an awareness hit me: I hadn't yet *fully* brought my own (EF) Executive Function and self-management online! I was still generating doubt within me. Did I really want to disempower myself by listening to my inner critic? Of course not. Bringing my own Executive Function fully online would require connecting with myself as never before. For me to thrive — not merely survive — I had to disengage faster from any mental process that could pull me into a negative or distracted thinking. In the deepest sense, I had to remember and feel who I was at a core nonverbal level. This is what I think most people are looking for, though each of us might describe it differently.

So here's my invitation to you. Whatever change you're considering or wrestling with, see if you can discern a block, obstacle or limiting thought that might be hiding out in *your* consciousness somewhere. Connect your *thoughts* about that change with what you're truly *feeling* about it. This means "following your gut."[67,68] From that connection, an *aha!* of some kind will emerge. Look for what you might possibly be embarrassed, ashamed or fearful about related to this change. That's the shadowy domain of the ego, which you can expose, clean out and move into history anytime. To do this, of course, you may have to dig for it with greater ownership and determination than ever before — but the freedom, joy and fulfillment you'll experience will be well worth it.

Each of us is given the potential to experience our lives in countless positive ways. We can either feel dedicated to going for what we want — or we can believe that life is "doing it to us" and keep coping. The number of moments in a day we feel gratitude or opportunity is up to each of us. As we've seen, we can accelerate our change from within in many ways: leaning into our discomfort, risking, revealing, getting support and sharing who we are. I hope it will be easier for you now, using what's in this book, and I urge you to share your progress. Take care of that precious gem within you that is your inner desire to grow. Protect, nourish, cherish, enjoy and listen to it as you navigate your own ocean of change, expanding continually into your own potential.

Feel free to connect with me, at: david@winkelmansolutions.com

CHAPTERS, PERSPECTIVES AND EXPLORATORY EXERCISES

PRESENTED BY PAGE NUMBER FOR EASY ACCESS

A VISIONARY END GAME

One of my many motivations for writing **Embracing Change** is to establish a context for creating a business model that has been gestating inside me since the mid 1980's. It's had a number of names. Currently it's: Connections: Urban Retreat & Studio.

The purpose of Connections: Urban Retreat & Studio is to facilitate desired behavior change quickly, thoroughly, predictably at the lowest possible cost for the greatest number of people, while creating greater community and well-being in the world.

As a business it will fully leverage technology and is based on genuine connection.

CONNECTIONS URBAN RETREAT & STUDIO. . .

is a personal and professional development center that will facilitate breakthrough and desired change[28] by creating the ideal conditions for supporting best qualities, and thus a potential for higher performance. CONNECTIONS is a distinctive learning and meeting space combined with a creative studio, where people can eat, meet and relax, be inspired, discover solutions, get support, make things happen. In addition to providing a unique and safe community of practice, it will offer: 1) highly-specialized creative spaces for rent; 2) membership; 3) retail sales from its own and others' services, programs, and products.

Imagine a space whose total design – everything you see, hear, touch, smell and sense, interaction, visualization, and every detail – has been created and assembled to inspire and support people in fulfilling their personal and professional goals faster.

A CENTER FOR HUMAN DEVELOPMENT

Every year, millions of US adults and their employers invest time and money on services, products and programs that promise to help people make their lives better. These investments don't pay off when three variables are missing: 1) the right environment — generally the most difficult or costly of factors to control, change or create; 2) the quality of support people get for making the kind of change or growth they desire; 3) Actual tools or know-how that help enable people to make and sustain desired change.

Specially designed environments enabled these companies to achieve huge results.

1) They enhance the shopping experience while building brand.

2) They increase spending and high customer return.

3) They increase functionality, efficiency and productivity.

Answer to the Nine-Dots puzzle on page 126

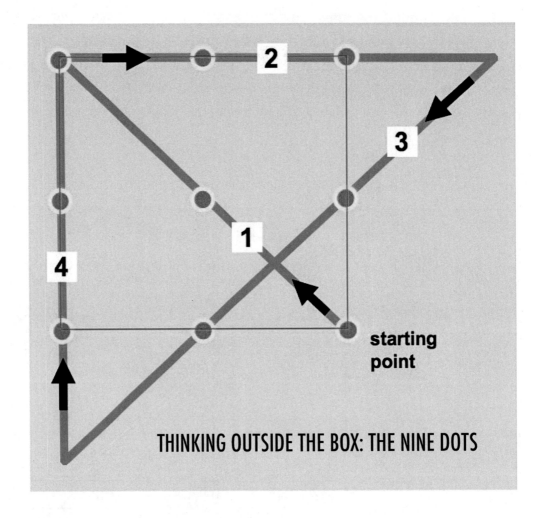

NOTES and APPENDICES

PAGE ii
1. According to Miriam Webster's online dictionary, the term gamechanger (defined as a newly introduced element or factor that changes an existing situation or activity in a significant way) was first noticed in 1993. It's become a common term that describes news makers of all type. I used the term in this book to describe one of five broad organizing principles through which we can grasp any complex situation. These elements are central to the process of achieving change of any kind; without them, the process of change will generally stall or go sideways.

Looking at the word "game" in the landscape of change, I want to acknowledge a wonderful parallel between my Five GameChanger characters and some of the characters in the book, *SuperBetter*, by well- known author, TED speaker and gamer, Jane McGonigal, which came out in 2015. In that year, I took off from my own writing process and was barely aware of her book. I discovered later that she uses the words: allies, bad guys, power-ups and ninjas. Jane, too, brings in the calvary, in a highly structured game-oriented way, with amazing detail, meticulous research and a brilliant track record in game analysis and design. If you like what I've laid out here, you might want to look at her book as well.

PAGE v
2. Throughout the book we look at various examples of leverage, a generally under-discussed critical success factor in life. Maximizing leverage is a foundation in finance, marketing and structural engineering. Cultivating leverage is an invaluable skill in achieving desired change both in and around you.

PAGE 2
3. Given most of our emotional responses are based on conscious and unconscious triggers, our emotional intelligence (EI or EQ) is largely built on awareness of one's own and others' trigger *patterns*. Regarding the word triggered (or triggers): Marshall Goldsmith, the #1 Executive Coach in the world, wrote a book in 2015 called *Triggers,* which validates a good deal of what's in *Embracing Change* and contains more detailed material.

4. While this is a term others may use, I'm more or less coining it here as far as I know.

PAGE 4
5. The real source of my anxiety was early childhood developmental trauma, which I was dissociating from. Dissociation is a mental mechanism by which a person to cuts himself off from his feelings and emotions, so that in effect, he doesn't feel the intensity of his feelings. Dissociation comes in many degrees of severity, from very mild to full blown, which would require hospitalization and medication.

6. By "intellectually", means I was highly articulate for my age. I had memorized the entire poem,"*The Night Before Christmas*" by age four though I hadn't learned to read. I loved to have answers for people, which continues into adulthood. Needless to say, the drive to be seen as intelligent is almost universal.
PAGE 5

7. The giant gap between the amount of feeling I had for *the world around me* versus the small amount of emotion I typically felt for myself was very disorienting for me for most of my life. I mistook intense thinking *about* things for having real, gut feelings *for myself.* This was a major, unconscious and long-lasting error in my perception. Eventually becoming aware of the difference (a shift in my perception) made a game changing difference to me.

8. There are many forms of emotional numbing, with and without the aid of external processes or substances. In my case I didn't need any outside help. In her well known TED talk, sociologist Brené Brown, http://www.ted.com/talks/brene_brown_on_vulnerability.html asserts that we cannot "selectively numb" only those emotions we don't want to feel. All our emotions are affected — good AND bad.

PAGE 6

9. Emotional hijacking and blind spots are described extensively by Daniel Goleman in his books, *Emotional Intelligence* and *Vital Lies, Simple Truths.* I believe he coined the phrase emotional hijacking.

10. Blind spots, also called lacunas, are very real, not just a figure of speech. Blind spots can be found at every level of society, from organizations of every size to regional cultures to individuals, couples and families.

11. My own working definition of a trauma is any negative life event that occurs in a condition of relative helplessness in which a person feels his survival is threatened. Early developmental childhood trauma is not acute or specific; it's gradual, there aren't specific events or incidents associated. "When we look at people like this, we find out that their bodies and their minds, their physiology and their brains, continue to behave and react to the world as if they're under siege, much as they were as kids. But there's no conscious connection between that and what is happening." *"What Neuroscience Teaches Us about the Treatment of Trauma"* (white paper/interview) with Ruth Buczynski, PhD and Bessel van der Kolk, MD. The National Institute for the Clinical Application of Behavioral Medicine www.nicabm.com

The specifics of my own childhood trauma aren't critical to the overall message of the book. The trauma I experienced had multiple sources, conditions that are probably more common today than are generally talked about: separation from my mother at birth (not by her choice), poor parenting, anger in the home, the divorce, anxiety all around me. What's noteworthy is the sense of survival — versus a sense of thriving — that the resulting trauma instilled in me — far outside my own awareness. Unrecognized and unhealed, such trauma conditions a brain to be on *high alert* — ever vigilant — so when anything that even looks like a threat is perceived, unconscious and automatic protective mechanisms get triggered. Such programs and mechanisms, well-disguised as adaptive and approval-seeking behaviors, acted on me from within for most of my life without my ever knowing. It was massive frustration (pain or the threat of it) that drove me to seek out answers and end the rationalizing to which I'd long grown accustomed. That's what's most dangerous about trauma, which isn't recognized, yet coped with insidious ways by the unconscious mind. One of the best books available on this subject is: Waking the Tiger: Healing Trauma by Peter Levine.

PAGE 8

12. Transformation has been described by countless thought leaders and authors. It's a subjective term that is best understood in the particular context in which it's being used, whether the communicator is an individual, consultant, leader, corporation, etc.

PAGE 9

13. At anytime you can make this a goal as well, preferably using the model of a Smart Goal — a well-established part of mainstream management vernacular. SMART stands for:

S for Specific – as in a particular result, object, behavior, event, attribute, etc.

M for Measurable – providing a clear indicator of change or progress

A for Achievable – reasonable given current time, money or talent resources

R for Relevant or Realistic – aligned with all the other goals in process

T for Timely – within a specific time frame or end date

PAGE 11

14." **Switch:** *How to Change Things When Change is Hard.* Chip & Dan Heath. page 6, The original elephant model was actually developed by University of Virginia psychologist Jonathan Haidt in his book, *The Happiness Hypothesis.*

PAGE 18

15. Buckminster Fuller developed numerous inventions, mainly architectural designs, and was the individual most responsible for bringing the geodesic dome into mainstream use around the world. He was a global teacher, inventor, and author of more than 30 books, who coined terms such as "Spaceship Earth", "synergetic" and "win-win" decades ago.

PAGE 23

16. A simple and useful way to understand management is to see it as the process of making activity predictable — and therefore results — *more predictable*, from machines to systems to individual and group behavior.

PAGE 24

17. Vulnerability means choosing to be selectively open about one's flaws, weaknesses and things we want to work on with people we respect and trust. It's the subject of Brené Brown's work in four books, one of the most-watched TED talks of all time, and her own certified training program for professionals.

18. YouTube of the song *"Let It Go"*: http://www.youtube.com/watch?v=L0MK7qz13bU

PAGE 29

19. Jobs is actually known for having and using what people around him affectionately called a "reality

distortion field"— his ability to push for a wild, creative idea or "impossible" goal which no one else could see until he finally convinced others of its merit and achievability. As documented in his biography by Walter Isaacson, this led to many out-of-the-box innovations.

PAGE 30

20. David and Goliath by Malcolm Gladwell, 2014, page 1-14.

PAGE 31

21. *Brain Rules, John Medina. Chapter 10 Vision, pages 221-240*

22. *My Stroke Of Insight, Jill Bolte-Taylor, Ph.D., page 19.* Link to video of her TED talk: http://www.ted.com/talks/jill_bolte_taylor_s_powerful_stroke_of_insight

PAGE 32

23. "Perceptual flexibility" which you might also find referred to as "cognitive flexibility" is a term I think you'll find in others' writings. In his book, *Social Intelligence* Daniel Goleman, discusses advanced neural imaging of perception and interpretation, on page 76, in the section ON SECOND THOUGHT. "By changing the meaning of what we perceive, we also alter its emotional impact. As Marcus Aurelius said millennia ago, pain 'is not due to the thing itself, but to your estimate of it, and this you have the power to revoke at any moment.'" Modern neuroscience is still working on understanding the entire and extraordinarily complex process of perception and accurately interpreting — making clear meaning — of what we sense.

PAGE 34

24. From the biography, *Steve Jobs*, by Walter Isaacson, page 337. Also reported in HBR: https://hbr.org/2012/04/the-real-leadership-lessons-of-steve-jobs

PAGE 41

25. From the website: Primary Goals.org   www.primarygoals.org/books/heart-of-change/gloves-on-boardroom-table/ Copyright © 2014 Education Theme on Genesis Framework.

PAGE 43

26. From the biography, *Steve Jobs*, by Walter Isaacson, page 371.

PAGE 44

27. From the inside dust cover of the book, *To The Desert and Back: The Story of One of the Most Dramatic Business Transformations on Record*, 2003. Philip Mirvis, Keren Ayas and George Roth,

PAGE 45

28. Fukushima Daiichi nuclear disaster as reported in Wikipedia
29. As reported in the 2013 documentary *The Armstrong Lie*

30. Daniel Goleman. *Vital Lies, Simple Truths: The Psychology of Self-Deception.* original paperback edition. 1985. Touchstone Books/Simon & Schuster.

PAGE 47

31. https://en.wikipedia.org/wiki/Lewinsky_scandal

PAGE 51

32. I attribute this observation to *The 7 Habits of Highly Effective People* by Stephen Covey, in which Stephen has an entire chapter dedicated to personal vision. I was never actually able to find the exact quote after I'd written it down.

33. For a video interview of Airbnb founder Brian Chesky at Fortune Global Forum that tells the story, go to: http://bit.ly/1TDz7j0

PAGE 56

34. "Amazing Grace", written in 1773 by English poet and clergyman, John Newton, is essentially a song about a transformation in perception. According to Wikipedia, "Amazing Grace", is one of the most recognizable songs in the English-speaking world. Author Gilbert Chase writes that it is "without a doubt the most famous of all the folk hymns,"while Jonathan Aitken, a Newton biographer, estimates that it is performed about 10 million times annually. I'm not suggesting a shift in perception will spark a spiritual awakening, but a shift of one's strongly held point of view can usually work wonders.

PAGE 59

35. "A Chiseled Bodybuilder, Frail Clients and a Fitness Story for the Ages." New York Times. June 20, 2014, Louis Lazar. Sports Section. http://www.nytimes.com/2014/06/21/sports/a-chiseled-bodybuilder-now-shaping-frail-clients.html?_r=0

36. Arthur's Inspirational Transformation: http://ddpyoga.com/arthur.html

37. "Power of Words" video: https://www.youtube.com/watch?feature=playerembedded&v=Hzgzim5m7oU

38. *The Life We Are Given.* George Leonard and Michael Murphy. 2008.

PAGE 69

39. In his 1990 blockbuster book, *Flow: The Psychology of Optimal Experience,* author and psychologist Mihaly Csikszentmihalyi, Ph.D., famously described the state of "flow"— being completely immersed in a challenge over time. https://en.wikipedia.org/wiki/Flow_(psychology.) Flow might be considered the opposite of multitasking, which is prevalent in today's workplace. He also delivers a wonderful TED talk on the subject: https://www.ted.com/talks/mihaly_csikszentmihalyi_on_flow?language=en. *The Rise of Superman* by Steven Kotler, is a fabulous resource for anyone motivated to read more on this amazing subject.

40. Though the quote expresses a rather universal thought, in this case, "The way things are is the way

they're supposed to be," came from Enrique Godreau III, SVP of Development, UP Global, as reported from "Igniting a Sense of Startup Culture", 360° Magazine, Steelcase, Issue #70, pg. 117.

PAGE 72

41. Common or prevailing emotions in many workplaces (in my experience) are fear, arrogance, anger and resentment. Any of these can easily be masked with or by taking control or expressions of defensiveness, passive-aggressiveness, or other covert patterns.

42. A SWOT Analysis – which stands for Strengths Weaknesses Opportunities Threats, is a common method of situation assessment using multiple points of view. A SWOT analysis can be done as casually as on a napkin or in a robust, formal, systematic, collaborative way, and there are as many forms of them as people who do them. SWOT analyses are useful tools that give people permission to air their concerns in depth without fear of reprisal or judgment.

PAGE 80

43. I am a Certified Trainer of Emotional Intelligence (EQ) with TalentSmart, the largest provider of corporate EQ training in the world. One of the things I love most to do in the world is to conduct EQ trainings, especially when senior management is solidly behind the program and doesn't view it as the "flavor of the month" kind of offering. (see: www.TalentSmart.com)

44. http://www.talentsmart.com/articles/How-Do-You-Stack-Up–EQ-Trends-by-Industry-41897549-p-1.html

PAGE 82

45. Oprah Winfrey's Wikipedia article: https://en.wikipedia.org/wiki/Oprah_Winfrey

46. Ropes courses, consisting of fun, memorable and challenging low-risk outdoor activities, are popular team and character building programs used widely by corporations, churches, camps, etc. The activities seem scary and often confrontive to participants., but there is seldom real danger for serious injury. Still, there is plenty of room for perceiving danger or failure if participants don't take some very real perceived risks.

PAGE 87

47. The Power of Place: by *Winifred Gallagher: How Our Surroundings Shape Our Thoughts, Emotions, and Actions,* 2007. page 126

PAGE 93

48. Impressive and fascinating research findings about motivation in the form of Dan Pink's TED talk: http://www.ted.com/talks/dan_pink_on_motivation#t-635240, which is based on his book, *A Whole New Mind.*

PAGE 98

49. The dance can be found at: https://www.youtube.com/watch?v=UqVB638qHfl
50. Arthur's story can be found at: http://ddpyoga.com/arthur.html

PAGE 99

51. Whole-hearted living, which ground a willingness to be appropriately vulnerable, is one of the central themes in at least Brené Brown's four major books.

PAGE 100

52. Mel Robbins: http://tedxtalks.ted.com/video/How-To-Stop-Screwing-Yourself-0

PAGE 102

53. Internal dialogue ("dialogical self" – https://en.wikipedia.org/wiki/Dialogical_self) has been given many names over many years — from writers, to gurus to neuroscientists: self-talk, endless chatter, mental noise, yadda-yadda, yammer-yammer and monkey mind to name a few.

PAGE 103

54. *What To Say When You Talk To Yourself*. Shad Helmstetter, Ph.D. 1982. page 35. He further comments on page 21 that: "Leading behavioral researchers have told us that as much as 77 percent of everything we think is negative, counterproductive and works against us."

PAGE 104

55. The Proprioceptive-Deep Tendon Reflex technique was developed by Dr. Jose Palomar. It's an extension of applied physiology, aka: muscle testing, which identifies blockages in the nervous system. http://www.drpalomar.com. One of Dr. Palomar's practitioners is Nathan Cohen, a wonderful Chiropractor in La Jolla. On my first visit to Nathan, I ended up crying hysterically for about ten minutes after the technique had released in me a deep holding pattern. I simply started feeling things I'd never allowed myself to feel before. One moment I was talking, the next moment I was blubbering — an experience I will never forget. The release, and resulting clarity from that release accelerated my progress significantly.

PAGE 107

56. Watch this one-minute 41 second video at: http://www.wimp.com/theego/. I don't know who produced this or what its exact purpose was originally. It's excellent, especially for it's short run time of 1:41.

PAGE 112

57. Regarding productivity and mindfulness: If you improve your overall state of well being, which includes your ability to focus and reduce the cumulative effects of stress, your productivity will increase, as hundreds of wellness and productivity research studies demonstrate. One of the best sources for mindfulness and meditation is the great Zen Master Thich Nhat Hanh, who has many YouTube videos, books, quotes, etc.

58. Amy Cuddy, who delivers the 2nd-highest-ranked TED talk: http://www.ted.com/talks/amy_cuddy_your_body_language_shapes_who_you_are, describes the conversion of presence to power in her 2016 book: *Presence: Bringing Your Boldest Self to Your Biggest Challenges*.
PAGE 113

59. The Search Inside Yourself Leadership Institute emerged several years ago from a Mindfulness and breathing awareness program offered to Google employees through Google University. It now stands on its own and is offered to corporations world-wide https://siyli.org

60. Please refer to my Conscious Breathing Experience at: http://winkelmansolutions.com/services/programs/ or contact me directly at: david@winkelmansolutions.com

PAGE 119

61. *The Life We Are Given.* George Leonard and Michael Murphy. 2008.

PAGE 126

62. This request is based on a prayer known internationally to the students of Indian teacher and spiritual leader Parmahansa Yogananda, who established the Self-Realization Fellowship with centers all over the world.

PAGE 133

63. *In Praise of Slowness.* Carol Honoré. 2004 Dust jacket cover notes.

PAGE 134

64. "The greatest good you can do for another is not just to share your riches, but to reveal to him his own." Benjamin Disraeli, (1804-1881), 2-time Prime Minister of England under Queen Victoria

PAGE 137

65. http://hbr.org/2001/12/primal-leadership-the-hidden-driver-of-great-performance/ar/pr

PAGE 138

66. American educator Helen Keller overcame the adversity of being blind, deaf and mute to become one of the 20th century's leading humanitarians, authors and educators.

PAGE 140

67. Following, trusting or listening to your guts, intuition, instincts, your body, etc., is critical. There is now a significant and growing body of neuroscientific evidence that in addition to the brain, we actually think with sensory mechanisms in our gut. The 2015 book *Gut: The Inside Story of Our Body's Most Underrated Organ*, by Giulia Enders, features a must-read chapter: "The Brain and the Gut," pages 122-142

68. For further insight into the strides made by neuroscience in the area of gut awareness and the direct links between thinking and feeling in our body, read *Social Intelligence* by Daniel Goleman. 2005. pages 82-99 in particular . . . and that was 10 years ago.

BIBLIOGRAPHY & RESOURCES (A partial listing)

EMOTIONAL INTELLIGENCE 2.0: Travis Bradberry & Jean Greaves

THE POWER OF HABIT: Why We Do What We Do in Life & Business John Duhigg

VITAL LIES, SIMPLE TRUTHS: The Psychology of Self Deception Daniel Goleman

EMOTIONAL INTELLIGENCE: Why It Can Matter More Than IQ Daniel Goleman

BRAIN RULES: 13 Principles for Thriving & Surviving at Work, Home & School John Medina

THE EXPERIENCE ECONOMY: Work Is Theatre & Every Business is a Stage Joe Pine & James Gilmore

SYNCHRONICITY: The Inner Path to Leadership Joe Jawarski

WHY WE BUY: The Science of Shopping Paco Underhill

THE LIFE WE ARE GIVEN: A Long-Term Program for Realizing the Potential of Body, Mind, Heart and Soul
Michael Murphy and George Leonard

THE CHARISMA EDGE: The How-to Guide for Turning On Your Leadership Power Cynthia Burnham

SWITCH: How to Change When Change Is Tough Chip Health and Dan Heath

IMMUNITY TO CHANGE: How to Overcome It and Unlock the Potential in Yourself and Your Organization
Robert Kegan and Lisa Laskow Lahey

NO-NONSENSE MANAGEMENT: A General Manager's Primer Richard Sloma

MY STROKE OF INSIGHT: A Brain Scientist's Personal Journey Jill Bolte-Taylor

THE ART OF EXPLANATION: Making Your Ideas Products and Services Easier to Understand Lee LeFever

MASTERING THE ROCKEFELLER HABITS: What You Must Do to Increase the Value of Your Fast-Growth Firm
Verne Harnish

MADE TO STICK: Why Some Ideas Survive and Others Die Chip Health and Dan Heath

IN SEARCH OF EXCELLENCE: Lessons From America's Best Run Companies Tom Peters & John A Waterman, Jr.

BLUR: The Speed of Change in the Connected Economy Stan Davis & Christopher Meyer

BUILT TO LAST: Successful Habits of Visionary Companies Jim Collins

UNLIMITED POWER: The New Science of Personal Achievement Anthony Robbins

THE WATCHMAN'S RATTLE: Thinking Our Way Out of Extinction Rebecca Costa

QUANTUM HEALING: Exploring the Frontiers of Mindy Body Medicine Deepak Chopra

SUPER BRAIN: Unleashing the Explosive Power of Your Mind to Maximize Health, Happiness & Spiritual Well-Being
        Deepak Chopra, M.D. & Rudolph Tanzi, Ph. D.

CRITICAL PATH: R. Buckminster Fuller

"WHAT NEUROSCIENCE TEACHES US ABOUT the TREATMENT OF TRAUMA"
        Webinar with Bessel van der Kolk, MD & Ruth Buczyniski, Ph.D
        National Institute for Clinical Application of Behavior Medicine (NICABM)

"PRIMAL LEADERSHIP": The Hidden Driver of Great Performance, Daniel Goleman, Richard Boyatzis &
        Annie McKee (Harvard Business Review)

HOW CAN I HELP? Stories and Reflections on Service Ram and Paul Gorman

MORE WONDERFULLY QUOTABLE PERSPECTIVES

"Think you've tried everything? I guarantee you haven't." Thomas Edison

"Imagination is more important than knowledge. Knowledge is limited to all we now know and understand, while imagination embraces the entire world, and all there ever will be to know and understand." Albert Einstein

"If you find yourself in a hole, the first thing to do is stop digging." Will Rogers, American Humorist

"Just because you took a bite out of a crap sandwich doesn't mean you have to finish it."
Tamara Star www.dailytransformations.com

"Don't judge yourself by your past. You don't live there anymore." Anonymous

"What lies behind us and what lies ahead of us are tiny matters compared to what lies within us."
Henry David Thoreau

"The day science begins to study non-physical phenomena it will make more progress in one decade than in all the centuries of its existence." Nikola Tesla (1856-1943)

"Life can be pulled by goals just as surely as it can be pushed by drives." Viktor Frankl

"You are where you are in your life because of what you believe is possible for you." Oprah

"All truth passes through three stages: First it is ridiculed. Second, it is violently opposed. Third, it is accepted as being self-evident." Arthur Schopenhauer, 19th Century German philosopher

"When asked: Would you rather work for change or just complain, 81 percent of respondents replied, 'Do I have to pick? This is hard.'" Anonymous, from a humorous poster

"Human beings always do the most intelligent thing...after they've tried every other alternative and none of them have worked." R. Buckminster (Bucky) Fuller (developer of the geodesic dome)

LETTING THINGS GO AS A BEST PRACTICE — THE WHY OF IT

It always helps to boil down what's essential in order to communicate a clear message. While boiling things down may not strike you as one of life's essential functions, it involves an activity which happens to be a core metabolic function: *letting things go*, or in biological terms: elimination. Whether you think of this process as a pleasure or a pain, in order to be effective, eliminating what we *don't want* is a process we're all much better off engaging in willingly and quickly.

So why is it that people predictably resist the act of letting something go? Perhaps it's because thinking about elimination is subconsciously and culturally avoided in our society. We used to call things no one could openly do or discuss *taboo*. But today, however we look at it, it's simply uncomfortable to discuss and not appealing in general conversation. Certainly elimination doesn't get the kind of attention that other life functions (like consumption, production, creation, or locomotion) receive; but maybe it needs to. In practical terms, the failure to eliminate regularly and thoroughly can be an underlying and unidentified cause of illness and dysfunction, not to mention a lot of stress. We're not just talking about poop here, either. We could be talking about an employee, a customer or a policy that is no longer good for us.

Whether we're talking about our bodies, habits, closets, files, computers, clogged drains, or memories that no longer serve us, the more we clean out what isn't necessary, the greater our movement, the healthier and more functional we are, and the better we feel. Pollution is elimination gone awry and it's not healthy for any of us.

Another perspective about how essential elimination is to our health can be seen in the very act of breathing. Respiration is one-third intake of air, one-third absorption and one-third exhalation: the elimination of the waste product, carbon dioxide. We literally cannot live without eliminating the waste product carbon dioxide that results from our every breath.

Given that good elimination is in most people's best interests, how much more could we celebrate it, teach it, build it into our infrastructure, etc? While it's highly functional that many communities have implemented widespread recycling, what about making elimination a more natural (if not celebrated) element in our everyday thinking and daily conversation?

The faster we eliminate what we don't need or want, the better off we are in almost every area of our lives. As simple as this may sound — it's often the most difficult thing to do. The practical path is to get support from others for letting go and eliminating whatever might be holding us back. When we consider our potential for greater fulfillment by eliminating some of our negative or limiting thoughts and beliefs, elimination may be a more compelling path to success.

As creatures of habit in our families, organizations and communities get attached to their ways, ideas, perceptions, and beliefs, even their junk. Most organizations are challenged on a variety of fronts – including decision-making. When we're challenged to move forward, you can bet an underlying issue is letting go of something; and often that is the illusion of safety, comfort and security — a belief about "the way it is or needs to be."

What would YOU be better off letting go of today? Can you let it go or begin to? How far can you go? ***Let's practice this together throughout our lives.***

DAVID WINKELMAN'S ABBREVIATED BIO

David's thirty-plus year career in professional management has integrated a broad spectrum of industries, from Fortune 100's to family-run companies. In addition to consulting roles, his full-time positions have included: General Manager, Director and VP of Marketing & Operations. He has helped facilitate over 100 corporate strategic planning and team-building events and has staffed MG Taylor "Navigation Centers TM" for NASA, Greater Metropolitan Health Systems, and Ernst & Young, LLP. He served on the E&Y Boeing DesignShop team that launched the Dreamliner initiative in 1997.

Organizations with whom he's worked include: Boeing, Toyota Motors, Coca Cola, Johnson & Johnson, Kellogg, NASA, Genentech, Solar Turbines, Ernst & Young, MG Taylor, British Petroleum, HP, Xerox, VR Corp (The North Face), GLG Councils, two national insurance companies, and many more. Details can be found on: www.winkelmansolutions.com

In addition to being an expert meeting facilitator, David delivers custom programs that develop greater teamwork, productivity, emotional intelligence and wellness. He also designs infographics, frequently consults with clients on messaging, and is a published photographer.

To engage David's support for change, for you and/or your team, please contact him directly via email: david@winkelmansolutions.com, or visit his website: www.winkelmansolutions.com

Michael Blackwood

Made in the USA
San Bernardino, CA
20 October 2016